POPAI

THE 36th MERCHANDISING AWARDS

POINT
of
PURCHASE

DESIGN ANNUAL 2

RETAIL REPORTING CORPORATION • NEW YORK

Retail Reporting Corporation
302 Fifth Avenue
New York, NY 10001

Distributors to the trade in the United States and Canada
Van Nostrand Reinhold
115 Fifth Avenue
New York, NY 10003

Distributed outside the United States and Canada
Hearst Books International
1350 Avenue of the Americas
New York, NY 10019

Library of Congress Cataloging in Publication Data:
Main entry under the title: Point of Purchase Design Annual / 2

Printed and Bound in Hong Kong
ISBN 0-934590-64-3

Editor-in-chief: William Zurynetz
Editor: Paul Sigler
Designed by: Bernard Schleifer

CONTENTS

INTRODUCTION

Each entrant in the contest was judged from an actual display. A case history detailed the merchandising objectives of each entry and listed available field results. Entries were evaluated on the basis of:
- (A) Effectiveness of the unit as a solution to the requirements set forth in the case history;
- (B) Originality of concept;
- (C) Excellence of design and engineering; and
- (D) Quality of reproduction and manufacture.

The 1993 merchandising award winners were selected by teams of judges drawn from the ranks of America's top brand marketers and retailers, judging outside of their respective industries.

Why an Indian?
Before the turn of the century, a wooden Indian, one of the earliest forms of P-O-P, stood in front of almost every cigar store in America. The merchandising awards are stylized versions of that cigar store Indian. Marketing case history information of award winners are included throughout the yearbook.

Gold OMA Awards
Displays that are judged the best in the industry receive gold statuettes. Gold awards were presented to the highest scoring units in each major industry category. Display producers and their clients received gold statuettes.

Silver OMA Awards
Silver awards were presented to the second highest scoring units in major industry categories. Display producers and clients received silver statuettes.

Bronze OMA Awards
Bronze statuettes were awarded to producers and clients of those units receiving outstanding scores by the judges.

Display of the Year
A blue-ribbon panel of marketing and retailing executives selected two display of the year winners in the permanent and promotional categories from all the gold winners. A special international judging team also selected the best promotional and permanent display to determine the winner of POPAI's International Display of the Year competition.

Sales Promotion of the Year
Teams of judges also selected the best sales promotion program to receive POPAI's Sales Promotion of the Year award. The winner was selected from the highest scoring units in the national and regional categories.

POINT
of
PURCHASE

DESIGN ANNUAL 2

The Clydesdale Parade was designed to be placed in a dominate position in key Budweiser retail outlets. The display was an attempt to update and contemporize the Budweiser Clydesdales, and reinforce their heritage and tradition. The display received strong wholesaler and retailer support and was placed in dominant and high visibility positions within the retailer's location.

The Parade helped in increasing sales and package distribution in most retail outlets. The unit cost $100 to $250 to produce and was constructed using injection molded plastic, metal, a motor, electric lamp and accessories.

The display was constructed by Lakeside, Ltd., Minneapolis, MN. It was intended for five years of use and had a production run of 2,500 units.

TITLE:
Budweiser Rotating Bowtie Clydesdale Spectacular

DIVISION:
Permanent

SUB-CAT:
On-Premise - Illuminated or Motion

CLIENT:
Anheuser-Busch, Inc.

ENTRANT:
Lakeside, Ltd.
Minneapolis, MN

AWARD:
Gold

TITLE:
Bucket of Buds Illuminated Sign

DIVISION:
Permanent

SUB-CAT:
On-Premise - Illuminated or Motion

CLIENT:
Anheuser-Busch, Inc.

ENTRANT:
Everbrite, Inc.,
Division - POP
Greenfield, WI

AWARD:
Silver

Red Stripe Jamaican Hut

DIVISION:
Permanent

SUB-CAT:
Off-Premise - Non-Illuminated or Non-Motion

CLIENT:
Labatt's USA

ENTRANT:
The Marketing Continuum, Inc.
Dallas, TX

AWARD:
Gold

Labatt's USA wanted to create an increased demand for their Red Stripe brand by 20% for the summer of 1993. The Marketing Continuum, Dallas, TX, created a display constructed of dried grass, plastic, wood, paper and chipboard to image fun and an island hut while still holding 50 cases of Red Stripe. The hut also was to increase the space the product received at retail making it more predominate. The display also featured a one-foot extension to the base to convert it into an on-premise mini-bar or booth.

After placement, sales were increased by an average of 56% through August of 1993. According to Labatt's the display also increased consumer awareness and interest in the Red Stripe brand.

The unit cost $50 to $100 dollars to construct and is expected to be used for three years.

TITLE:
Miller Genuine Draft "Ice Keg"

DIVISION:
Permanent

SUB-CAT:
On-Premise - Non-Illuminated or Non-Motion

CLIENT:
Miller Brewing Co.

ENTRANT:
Miller Brewing Co., Milwaukee, WI

AWARD:
Gold

TITLE:
Anheuser-Busch Natural Light Cooler Wall Hanging

DIVISION:
Permanent

SUB-CAT:
Off-Premise - Illuminated or Motion

CLIENT:
Anheuser-Busch, Inc.

ENTRANT:
**Thomas A. Schutz Co., Inc.
Morton Grove, IL**

AWARD:
Silver

The Ice Keg was used to reinforce the television ads representing the beer's draft beer taste and cold filtered image. The display also reinforced the brand's visibility and increased demand at the retail location. The display had to keep beer fresher and colder longer, and be very convenient to use.

Originally a production run of 25,000 was proposed but overwhelming demand along with consumer requests for the display pushed the production quantity to 170,000. Miller Brewing was the client and the maker of the display. They utilized injection molded, vacuum forming and post decoration. The unit has an intended use of one to two years, and costs $5 to $10 to construct.

Draft sales have increased by 50 to 250% at monitored location where the display was being utilized according to Miller Brewing.

Designed to be place in Sports Bars and Major League Sports venues, the Lite Sport Wall Sign set featured recognizable images for each sport. The display's cap replaces a ball or puck and immediately becoming part of the sport.

The signage had to be large, bold and intrusive, but not enough that the displays extruded too far as to interfere with bar patrons. Distorted perspectives were used to accomplish the effects. The displays could be used individually or as a set. Due to the positive reception, Miller Brewing extended the program into 1994, and will expand it to encompass other popular sporting events.

Designed by Lakeside, Ltd., of Minneapolis, MN, the program cost between $50 and $100 to build per unit with a use expectancy of three year. Vacuum formed plastic, injection molded plastic, masonite and metal were used in the construction of the signage.

TITLE:
Lite Sports Wall Sign Set

DIVISION:
Permanent

SUB-CAT:
On-Premise - Illuminated or Motion

CLIENT:
Miller Brewing Co.

ENTRANT:
Lakeside, Ltd.
Minneapolis, MN

AWARD:
Gold

TITLE:

Anheuser-Busch Sports Acrylic Tapmarker Family

DIVISION:

Permanent

SUB-CAT:

On-Premise - Non-Illuminated or Non-Motion

CLIENT:

Anhueser-Busch Companies, Inc.

ENTRANT:

Dorette Co.
Pawtucket, RI

AWARD:

Silver

TITLE:

Anheuser-Busch Budweiser and Budweiser
Light Major League

DIVISION:

Permanent

SUB-CAT:

On-Premise - Non-Illuminated or Non-Motion

CLIENT:

Anheuser-Busch Companies, Inc.

ENTRANT:

Dorette Co.
Pawtucket, RI

AWARD:

Bronze

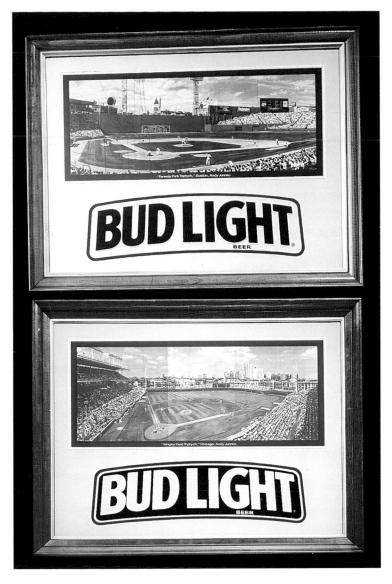

Bud Light Commemorative Baseball Deep Etched Mirrors

DIVISION:
Permanent

SUB-CAT:
On-Premise - Non-Illuminated or Non-Motion

CLIENT:
Anheuser-Busch, Inc.

ENTRANT:
**Beeco Manufacturing Co.
Chicago, IL**

AWARD:
Silver

TITLE:
Foster's In-Cooler

DIVISION:
Permanent

SUB-CAT:
Off-Premise - Illuminated or Motion

CLIENT:
Molson Breweries U.S.A.

ENTRANT:
**Wordenglass & Electricity, Inc.
Kalamazoo, MI**

AWARD:
Silver

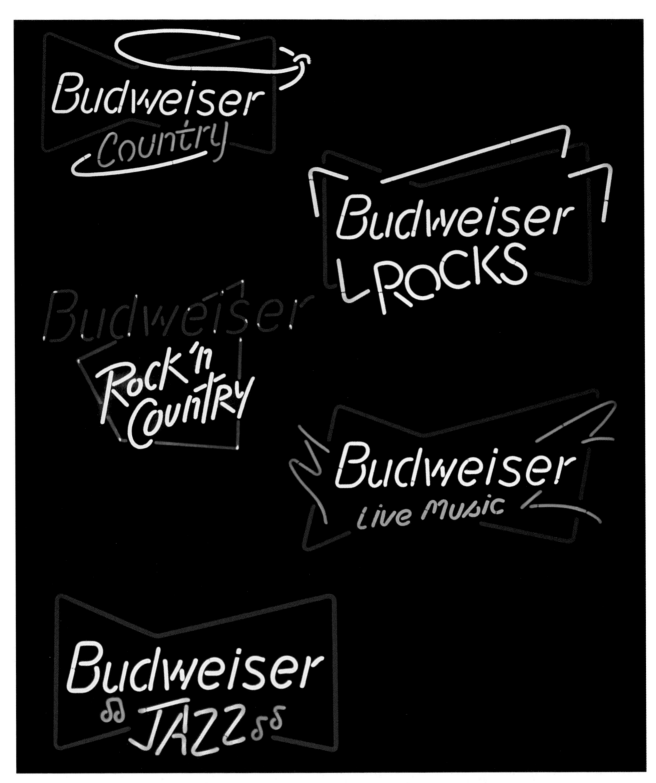

TITLE:
Budweiser "Live Music" Neon

DIVISION:
Permanent

SUB-CAT:
On-Premise - Illuminated or Motion

CLIENT:
Anheuser-Busch, Inc.

ENTRANT:
Everbrite, Inc.,
Division - POP
Greenfield, WI

AWARD:
Bronze

TITLE:

Budweiser Basketball Neon

DIVISION:

Permanent

SUB-CAT:

On-Premise - Illuminated or Motion

CLIENT:

Anheuser-Busch, Inc.

ENTRANT:

**Everbrite, Inc.,
Division - POP
Greenfield, WI**

AWARD:

Bronze

TITLE:

Coors Light Texas Music Neon

DIVISION:

Permanent

SUB-CAT:

On-Premise - Illuminated or Motion

CLIENT:

Coors

ENTRANT:

**Everbrite, Inc.,
Division - POP
Greenfield, WI**

AWARD:

Bronze

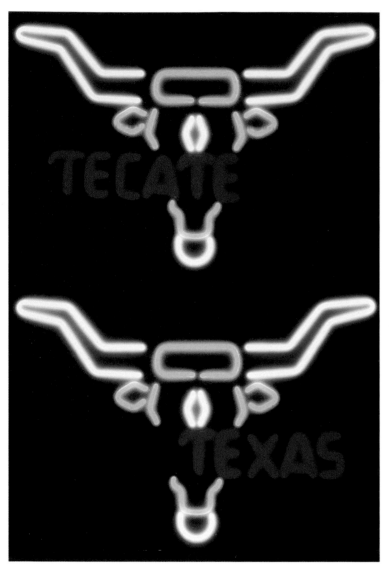

TITLE:
Tecate - Texas Steer

DIVISION:
Permanent

SUB-CAT:
On-Premise - Illuminated or Motion

CLIENT:
Wisdom Imports Sales Co.

ENTRANT:
**Everbrite, Inc.,
Subsidiary - GHN
Greenfield, WI**

AWARD:
Bronze

TITLE:
Lite Baseball Neon

DIVISION:
Permanent

SUB-CAT:
Off-Premise - Illuminated or Motion

CLIENT:
Miller Brewing Co.

ENTRANT:
**Everbrite, Inc.,
Division - POP
Greenfield, WI**

AWARD:
Bronze

Title:

Michelob Light Skier

DIVISION:

Permanent

SUB-CAT:

Off-Premise - Illuminated or Motion

CLIENT:

Anheuser-Busch, Inc.

ENTRANT:

**Everbrite, Inc.,
Subsidiary - GHN
Greenfield, WI**

AWARD:

Bronze

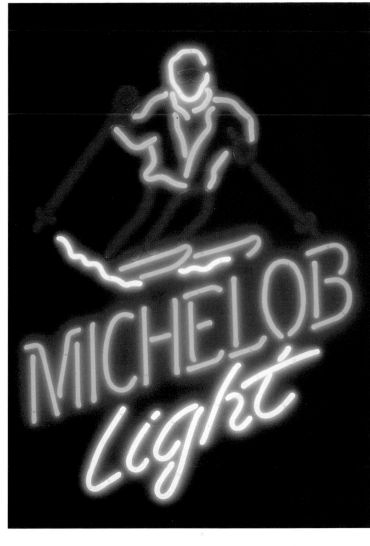

TITLE:

Miller Reserve - Saxophone

DIVISION:

Permanent

SUB-CAT:

On-Premise - Illuminated or Motion

CLIENT:

Miller Brewing Co.

ENTRANT:

**Everbrite, Inc.,
Subsidiary
Greenfield, WI**

AWARD:

Bronze

TITLE:

Budweiser Ski Tap Marker

DIVISION:

Permanent

SUB-CAT:

On-Premise - Non-Illuminated or Non-Motion

CLIENT:

Anheuser-Busch, Inc.

ENTRANT:

**Lakeside Ltd.
Minneapolis, MN**

AWARD:

Bronze

TITLE:

Coors Rodeo Tap Knob

DIVISION:

Permanent

SUB-CAT:

On-Premise - Non-Illuminated or Non-Motion

CLIENT:

Coors Brewing Co.

ENTRANT:

**Lakeside Ltd.
Minneapolis, MN**

AWARD:

Bronze

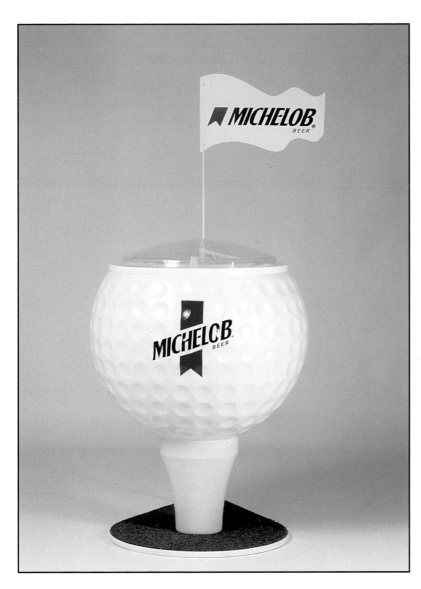

TITLE:

Michelob Golf Singles Cooler

DIVISION:

Permanent

SUB-CAT:

Off-Premise - Non-Illuminated or Non-Motion

CLIENT:

Anheuser-Busch Companies

ENTRANT:

Mead Merchandising
Atlanta, GA

AWARD:

Bronze

TITLE:

Miller Reserve Amber Ale Reception Lamp

DIVISION:

Permanent

SUB-CAT:

On-Premise - Illuminated or Motion

CLIENT:

Miller Brewing Co.

ENTRANT:

Trans World Marketing
East Rutherford, NJ

AWARD:

Bronze

TITLE:

Morietti Beer Neon

DIVISION:

Permanent

SUB-CAT:

On-Premise - Illuminated or Motion

CLIENT:

The Marketing Continuum, Inc.

ENTRANT:

**Everbrite, Inc.
Greenfield, WI**

AWARD:

Bronze

TITLE:

Lite Braves Tomahawk

DIVISION:

Permanent

SUB-CAT:

On-Premise - Illuminated or Motion

CLIENT:

Miller Brewing Co.

ENTRANT:

**Everbrite, Inc.,
Division - POP
Greenfield, WI**

AWARD:

Silver

TITLE:

Rolling Rock Logo Neon

DIVISION:

Permanent

SUB-CAT:

On-Premise - Illuminated or Motion

CLIENT:

The Marketing Continuum, Inc.

ENTRANT:

**Everbrite, Inc.,
Division - POP
Greenfield, WI**

AWARD:

Bronze

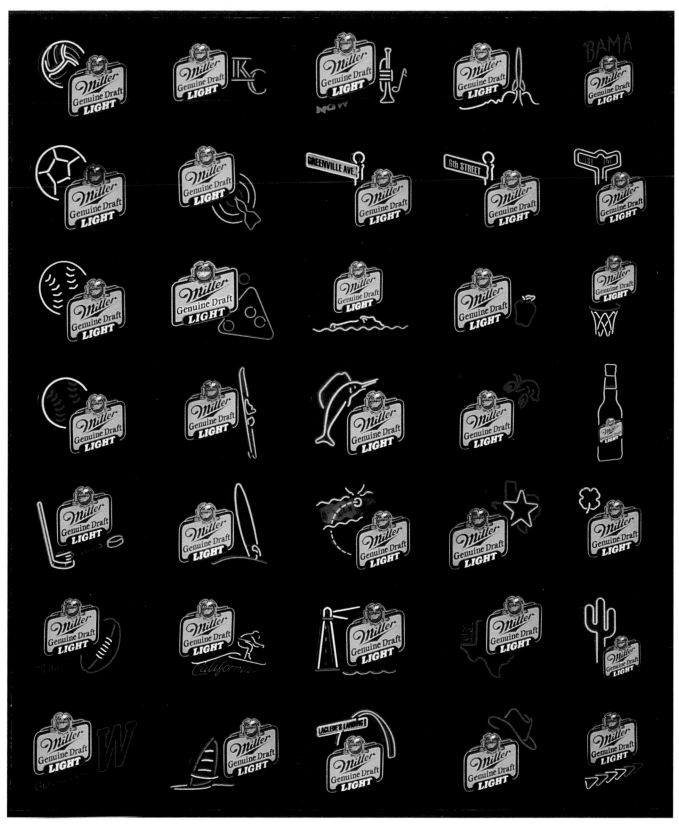

TITLE:
Miller GDL "Flex" Neon Program

DIVISION:
Permanent

SUB-CAT:
On-Premise - Illuminated or Motion

CLIENT:
Miller Brewing Co.

ENTRANT:
**Everbrite, Inc.,
Division - POP
Greenfield, WI**

AWARD:
Bronze

TITLE:
Budweiser/Wrigley Field Talking Sign

DIVISION:
Temporary

SUB-CAT:
Off-Premise - Illuminated or Motion

CLIENT:
Anheuser-Busch, Inc.

ENTRANT:
**Visual Marketing, Inc.
Chicago, IL**

AWARD:
Gold

As a sponsor of Cubs baseball, Anheuser-Busch, Inc. wanted to create customer recall to both the team and the company. The talking display featured a message from a famous announcer that greeted customers in Chicago area liquor outlets.

The sign was a replica of the entrance sign at Wrigley Field. A volume control on the voice box allowed retailers to raise or lower the message as needed. A traveling message privilege panel, which can be converted to a pricing area, also is part of the display. Changeable dot matrix package inserts were supplied to retailers so weekly specials could be advertised.

The sign is constructed of an 80 pound enamel printing mounted to a 50 point board. The sign could be wall mounted by repositioning the sensor into the corrugated platform inside and removing die-cut holes for the sensor and voice. Designed by Visual Marketing, Chicago, IL, the unit cost between $50 and $100 to produce and had a production run of 1,000. It was intended for use during the 1993 baseball season.

TITLE:

Lite NFL Inflatable Helmet Dangler

DIVISION:

Temporary

SUB-CAT:

Off-Premise - Non-Illuminated or Non-Motion

CLIENT:

Miller Brewing Co.

ENTRANT:

Alvimar Mfg. Co., Inc.
Long Island City, NY

AWARD:

Bronze

TITLE:

Pabst Bottle Glorifier

DIVISION:

Permanent

SUB-CAT:

On-Premise - Illuminated or Motion

CLIENT:

Pabst Brewing Co.

ENTRANT:

Process Displays, Inc.
New Berlin, WI

AWARD:

Bronze

TITLE:
Budweiser Memorial Day Motion Spectacular/Anheuser-Busch

DIVISION:
Temporary

SUB-CAT:
Off-Premise - Illuminated or Motion

CLIENT:
Anheuser-Busch, Inc.

ENTRANT:
Rapid Mounting and Finishing Co.
Chicago, IL

AWARD:
Bronze

TITLE:
Coors Extra Gold Light Back Bar Glorifier

DIVISION:
Temporary

SUB-CAT:
On-Premise - Illuminated or Motion

CLIENT:
Adolph Coors Co.

ENTRANT:
Advertising Display Co.
Englewood Cliffs, NJ

AWARD:
Gold

TITLE:
Zima Bottle Replica Floor Display Program

DIVISION:
Temporary

SUB-CAT:
Off-Premise - Non-Illuminated or Non-Motion

CLIENT:
Coors Brewing Co.

ENTRANT:
Henschel-Steinau, Inc.
Englewood, NJ

AWARD:
Silver

The back bar glorifier was designed to promote Coors new product Coors Extra Gold Light. It made a dramatic presentation of Coors new product by using two vacuum formed parts and silk screened in seven colors. Constructed by Advertising Display Company, Englewood, NJ, it had a production run of 3,200 and a cost of under $5 per unit.

The glorifier's opaque distortion-printed plastic bottle is illuminated from behind by an electric bulb. It has a silver Mylar backing that accentuates the reflectivity of the light. With a use expectancy of six months, the display was "very effective" in promoting the new product.

TITLE:
O'Doul's Bottle Cap Clock

DIVISION:
Permanent

SUB-CAT:
On-Premise - Illuminated or Motion

CLIENT:
Anheuser-Busch, Inc.

ENTRANT:
Lakeside, Ltd
Minneapolis, MN

AWARD:
Bronze

TITLE:
Miller Reserve Christmas Stacker

DIVISION:
Temporary

SUB-CAT:
Off-Premise - Non-Illuminated or
Non-Motion

CLIENT:
Miller Brewing Co.

ENTRANT:
Menasha Corp.,
Color Division
Menomonee Falls, WI

AWARD:
Silver

TITLE:
Stroh's Pool Table Lamp

DIVISION:
Permanent

SUB-CAT:
On-Premise - Illuminated or Motion

CLIENT:
The Stroh Brewing Co.

ENTRANT:
Chicago Show
Morton Grove, IL

AWARD:
Bronze

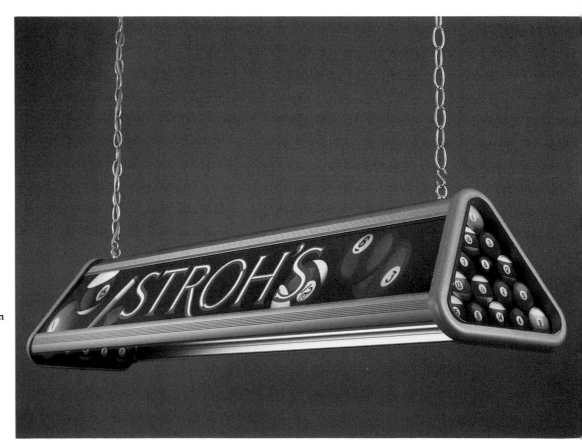

TITLE:
Pabst "Customized" Deep Etched Mirror

DIVISION:
Permanent

SUB-CAT:
On-Premise - Non-Illuminated or Non-Motion

CLIENT:
Pabst Brewing Co.

ENTRANT:
**Beeco Manufacturing Co.
Chicago, IL**

AWARD:
Bronze

TITLE:
Michelob Golf Motion Display

DIVISION:
Permanent

SUB-CAT:
On-Premise - Illuminated or Motion

CLIENT:
Anheuser-Busch, Inc.

ENTRANT:
**Lakeside, Ltd.
Minneapolis, MN**

AWARD:
Bronze

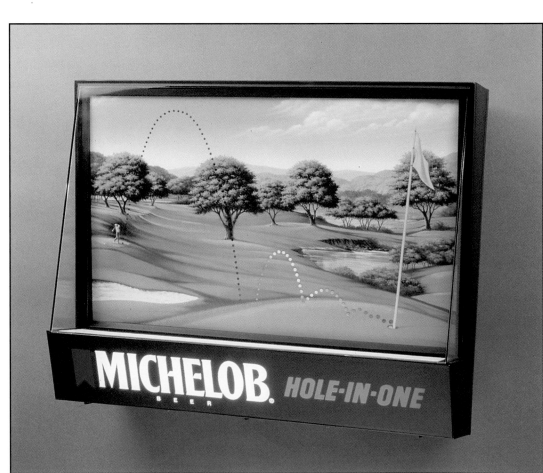

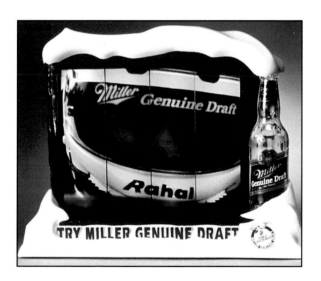

TITLE:

Tri-Vision Backbar Sign

DIVISION:

Permanent

SUB-CAT:

On-Premise - Illuminated or Motion

CLIENT:

Miller Brewing Co.

ENTRANT:

**Everbrite, Inc.,
Division - POP
Greenfield, WI**

AWARD:

Bronze

TITLE:
Miller Genuine Draft "Ice Keg" Promotion

DIVISION:
Temporary

SUB-CAT:
On-Premise - Non-Illuminated or Non-Motion

CLIENT:
Miller Brewing Co.

ENTRANT:
Miller Brewing Co.
Milwaukee, WI

AWARD:
Silver

TITLE:
Michelob Keg on Ice Motion Display

DIVISION:
Temporary

SUB-CAT:
Off-Premise - Illuminated or Motion

ENTRANT:
Anheuser-Busch, Inc.
St. Louis, MO

AWARD:
Bronze

TITLE:
Michelob Golden Draft Motion Fluted Can Display

DIVISION:
Temporary

SUB-CAT:
Off-Premise - Illuminated or Motion

CLIENT:
Anheuser-Busch, Inc.

ENTRANT:
The Dyment Co.
Cincinnati, OH

AWARD:
Bronze

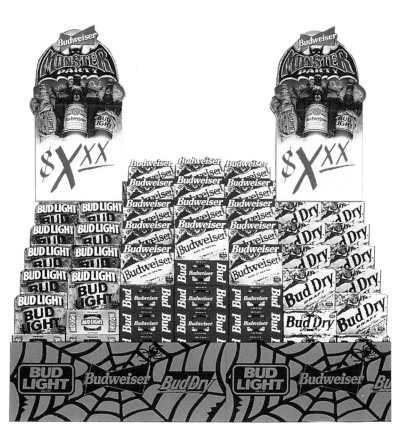

TITLE:

Bud Halloween

DIVISION:

Temporary

SUB-CAT:

On-Premise - Non-Illuminated or Non-Motion

CLIENT:

Anheuser-Busch, Inc.

ENTRANT:

Anheuser-Busch, Inc.
St. Louis, MO

AWARD:

Bronze

TITLE:

Michelob Golf

DIVISION:

Temporary

SUB-CAT:

On-Premise - Non-Illuminated or Non-Motion

CLIENT:

Anheuser-Busch, Inc.

ENTRANT:

Jefferson Sumrfit Corporation,
Tri-Pack Division
Chicago, IL

AWARD:

Silver

TITLE:
Schenley Pinch Deluxe Display

DIVISION:
Permanent

SUB-CAT:
Distilled Spirits - Non-Illuminated or Non-Motion

CLIENT:
Schieffelin & Somerset

ENTRANT:
**The Niven Marketing Group
Elk Grove Village, IL**

AWARD:
Bronze

Smirnoff's Citrus Twist has a similar label design as other Smirnoff products. The goal of the display was to align the product with the Smirnoff family, however it had to create brand awareness.

A back bar glorifier was designed by Harvey Shayew, Inc., Bay Shore, NY, utilizing vibrant green and yellow colors. The bottle and Smirnoff "Eyebrow" logo are both illuminated. The bottle outline also is silhouetted in a fluorescent green.

Constructed of lucite, styrene, mirrored styrene, an electrical harness utilizing vacuum forming fabrication and assembly, the unit had a production run of 525. The display had a production cost of $25 to $50 per unit.

TITLE:

Smirnoff Citrus Twist Lighted Back Bar Glorifier

DIVISION:

Permanent

SUB-CAT:

Distilled Spirits - Illuminated or Motion

CLIENT:

John G. Martin Div.

ENTRANT:

Harvey Shayew, Inc.
Bay Shore, NY

AWARD:

Gold

TITLE:

Captain Morgan Wood Display

DIVISION:

Permanent

SUB-CAT:

Distilled Spirits - Non-Illuminated or Non-Motion

CLIENT:

The House of Seagram

ENTRANT:

Ruszel Woodworks, Inc.
Benicia, CA

AWARD:

Silver

TITLE:
Jim Beam Holiday Motion Display

DIVISION:
Temporary

SUB-CAT:
Distilled Spirits - Illuminated or Motion

CLIENT:
Jim Beam Brands Co.

ENTRANT:
**Rapid Mounting and Finishing Co.
Chicago, IL**

AWARD:
Bronze

TITLE:
Old Grand-Dad Holiday

DIVISION:
Temporary

SUB-CAT:
Distilled Spirits - Illuminated or Motion

CLIENT:
Jim Beam Brands Company

ENTRANT:
**Rapid Mounting and Finishing
Chicago, IL**

AWARD:
Bronze

Created by Visual Marketing of Chicago, IL, for House of Seagrams, the program was created to promote individual drinks in lounges and restaurants, and as a floor merchandiser for off-premises retail outlets for the 20-year-old wood-aged Crown Royal Special Reserve whiskey. The display was needed to obtain distribution, secure permanent space, generate consumer awareness, trial and impulse purchase.

The display featured an oak wood background with mirror finished gold plastic with an injection molded logo name plate. The off unit display featured a 12-bottle merchandiser made primarily of oak. The logo identification on the sides of the display used a thermo engraved brass plate.

At a cost for production of $100 to $250 and use expectancy of six months for the floor display and one year for the back bar display, 400 floor and 1,200 back bar units were produced. The program was successful in promoting the high quality image the Crown Royal line represents.

TITLE:
Seagrams Crown Royal Special Reserve Program

DIVISION:
Permanent

SUB-CAT:
Distilled Spirits - Illuminated or Motion

CLIENT:
House of Seagrams

ENTRANT:
**Visual Marketing, Inc.
Chicago, IL**

AWARD:
Gold

Schieffelin & Somerset needed a display that elegantly featured the Johnnie Walker Black Label in a traditional holiday theme. Motion also had to be incorporated with a variety of shapes and textures to attract attention to the product. The ultimate goal was to increase sales volume of the top shelf brand.

Constructed to be used for the 1993/1994 holiday season, the display had favorable response from retailers. The display was produced by Silverado & Company, Inc., New York, NY. It was produced in a quantity of 3,500 at a cost of $25 to $50 per unit.

TITLE:

Johnnie Walker Black Label Holiday Motion Sled

DIVISION:

Temporary

SUB-CAT:

Distilled Spirits - Illuminated or Motion

CLIENT:

Schieffelin & Somerset Co.

ENTRANT:

Silverado & Company, Inc.
New York, NY

AWARD:

Gold

TITLE:

Glenlivet Shelf System

DIVISION:

Permanent

SUB-CAT:

Distilled Spirits - Non-Illuminated or Non-Motion

CLIENT:

The House Of Seagrams

ENTRANT:

P.O.P., Inc.
Long Island City, NY

AWARD:

Silver

TITLE:
Cutty Sark Dimensional Neon Sign

DIVISION:
Permanent

SUB-CAT:
Distilled Spirits - Illuminated or Motion

CLIENT:
Hiram Walker & Sons, Inc.

ENTRANT:
Visual Marketing, Inc.
Chicago, IL

AWARD:
Bronze

TITLE:
Cutty Sark Holiday Fireplace Display

DIVISION:
Temporary

SUB-CAT:
Distilled Spritis - Non-Illuminated or Non-Motion

CLIENT:
Hiram Walker & Sons, Inc.

ENTRANT:
Bish Creative Display
Lake Zurich, IL

AWARD:
Silver

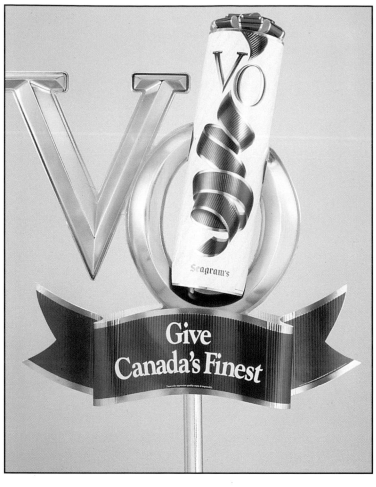

TITLE:

Give Canada's Finest - Motion Pole Display - Nov/Dec 1993

DIVISION:

Temporary

SUB-CAT:

Distilled Spirits - Illuminated or Motion

CLIENT:

Joseph E. Seagram & Sons

ENTRANT:

**Joseph E. Seagram & Sons
The House of Seagram
New York, NY**

AWARD:

Bronze

TITLE:

Tott's Mini Mass Display

DIVISION:

Temporary

SUB-CAT:

Cordials and Wines

CLIENT:

E. & J. Gallo Winery

ENTRANT:

**Bert-Co Graphics
Dublin, CA**

AWARD:

Bronze

TITLE:
Goldschläger Back-Bar Glorifier

DIVISION:
Temporary

SUB-CAT:
Distilled Spirits - Illuminated or Motion

CLIENT:
The Paddington Corp.

ENTRANT:
**Display Masters
Long Island City, NY**

AWARD:
Silver

TITLE:
"The Legendary Gift" Motion Pole Display

DIVISION:
Temporary

SUB-CAT:
Distilled Spirits - Illuminated or Motion

CLIENT:
Joseph E. Seagram & Sons

ENTRANT:
**Joseph E. Seagram & Sons
The House of Seagram
New York, NY**

AWARD:
Silver

 THE SURREY INSTITUTE OF ART & DESIGN

Farnham Campus, Falkner Road, Farnham, Surrey GU9 7DS

TITLE:

Baileys/Baileys Light Irish Cream Holiday Program

DIVISION:

Temporary

SUB-CAT:

Distilled Spirits - Illuminated or Motion

CLIENT:

The Paddington Corporation

ENTRANT:

Harvey Shayew, Inc.
Bay Shore, NY

AWARD:

Bronze

TITLE:

Georgia Moon Corn Whiskey Counter Display

DIVISION:

Temporary

SUB-CAT:

Distilled Spirits - Non-Illuminated or Non-Motion

CLIENT:

Heaven Hill Distilleries

ENTRANT:

Henschel-Steinau, Inc.
Englewood, NJ

AWARD:

Bronze

TITLE:
The Chivas Regal of Gifts - Motion Pole Display

DIVISION:
Temporary

SUB-CAT:
Distilled Spirits - Illuminated or Motion

CLIENT:
Joseph E. Seagram & Sons

ENTRANT:
Joseph E. Seagram & Sons
The House of Seagram
New York, NY

AWARD:
Gold

Intended for use during November and December, 1993, the motion pole display's goal was to establish floor dominance and visibility in the holiday environment. Joseph E. Seagram and Sons wanted to increase the sales of 1.75L, 1L and 750ml sizes of Chivas Regal, as well as promote a value-added holiday gift pack with the display.

Constructed by Seagram, the display utilized foil, corrugation, embossing, mounting and finishing. The display featured five 1.75L gift cartons, and a prominent gift tag pronouncing Chivas as the ultimate holiday gift. The display had a suggested nine to 15 case stacking capability to draw attention to it in the retail environment.

The unit cost $50 to $100 to produce with a total of 2,550 units constructed.

TITLE:
Multi-Brand Display

DIVISION:
Permanent

SUB-CAT:
Cordials and Wines

CLIENT:
Hiram Walker & Sons, Inc.

ENTRANT:
IDL, Inc.
Pittsburgh, PA

AWARD:
Silver

TITLE:
Jose Cuervo Gift Shipper

DIVISION:
Temporary

SUB-CAT:
Distilled Spirits - Non-Illuminated or Non-Motion

CLIENT:
Heublein, Inc.

ENTRANT:
Stone Container Corp.
Richmond, VA

AWARD:
Bronze

TITLE:
Dunnewood Wire Rack

DIVISION:
Permanent

SUB-CAT:
Cordials and Wines

CLIENT:
Canandaigua Wine Company

ENTRANT:
Rand Display, Inc.
Englewood Cliffs, NJ

AWARD:
Silver

TITLE:

Marcus James Injection Molded Rack

DIVISION:

Temporary

SUB-CAT:

Cordials and Wines

CLIENT:

Canandaigua Wine Company

ENTRANT:

Rand Display, Inc.
Englewood Cliffs, NJ

AWARD:

Silver

TITLE:

Olmeca Tequila Promotional Displays

DIVISION:

Permanent

SUB-CAT:

Distilled Spirits – Non-Illuminated or Non-Motion

CLIENT:

House of Seagram

ENTRANT:

Acrylic Designs, Inc.
Springfield, VT

AWARD:

Bronze

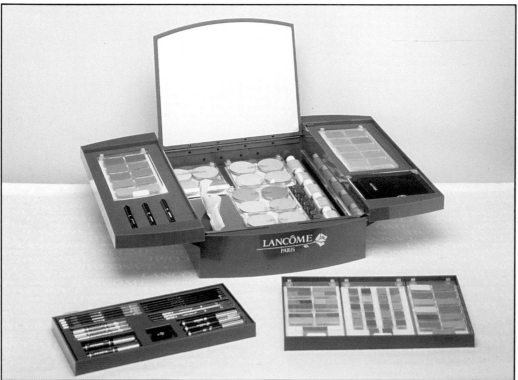

TITLE:
Lancome "Beaute a La Carte"
Make-up Candy

DIVISION:
Permanent

SUB-CAT:
Multiple Product Line Merchandisers

CLIENT:
Lancome, Inc.

ENTRANT:
Shannen Promotions, Inc.
New York, NY

AWARD:
Silver

Halston/Borghese needed a display for department stores, select drug stores and chemists that would create a color center not only for test products, but would display the eye, lip and face color in predetermined combinations. The display also, if possible, allows the consumer or consultant the ability to mix and match colors from one wardrobe to another and return to the predetermined wardrobe after each use.

Dauman Displays of New York, NY, constructed a display utilizing injection molding fabricated acrylic sheets, die stamping, vacuum forming, illumination and motion. The display had to have a useful life of three to five years and a production run of 2,000. It would cost over $500 per unit to produce.

The display features over 50 wardrobes with testing of one live color from each wardrobe plus live testing of 41 additional lip colors. It also glorifies two makeup products and two lipstick cases. The display rotates 150 degrees in each direction to allow the consumer to see how the lip color on one ring goes with the face color on another. A mechanical device allows the display to be turned by hand, but holds them in place for 23 seconds after the disc is release. The disc is then returned to the original preset position.

The unit has all eye, lip and face colors on the face of the display and housed in removable cassettes for easy updating. On the rear of the unit there are 11 removable tester drawers which contain face, cheek, lip and eye products held in updatable vacuum formed inserts. There also are 27 additional lipsticks on the rear of the unit.

TITLE:	TITLE:
Estee Fruition Tester	**Borghese Color Center**
DIVISION:	DIVISION:
Permanent	**Permanent**
SUB-CAT:	SUB-CAT:
Testers	**Testers**
CLIENT:	CLIENT:
Estee Lauder, Inc.	**Halston/Borghese**
ENTRANT:	ENTRANT:
IDMD Manufacturing, Inc. **Scarborough, ONT, Canada**	**Dauman Displays** **New York, NY**
AWARD:	AWARD:
Gold	**Gold**

Estee Lauder needed a display that would promote a new treatment product, but would allow the customer to test the product, take limited counter space and be pilfer proof. IMD Manufacturing, Scarborough, ONT, Canada, constructed a display utilizing cast acrylic, anodized aluminum, fabrication, thermo forming and silk screening. Three thousand units would be constructed at a cost of $50 to $100 per unit. It would be used for a period of one year.

By using a frosted material backed-up with a mirror image the display catches the colors of the new product. Three-dimensional collage effect emphasizing the product and helped to achieve the visual impact. The display used an interlocking system where the pump was exposed by the bottle, but was not removable except by the advisor. A caddy built into the back of the display holds additional product, cotton balls and applicators.

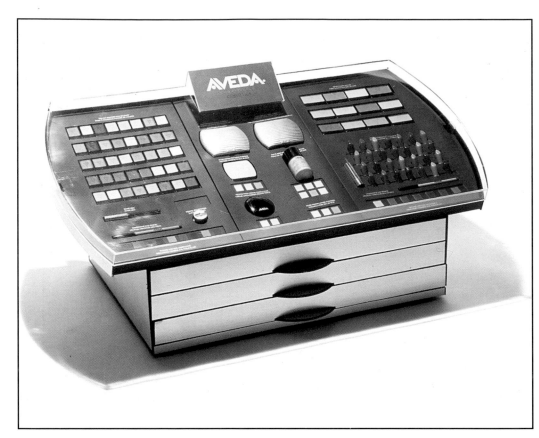

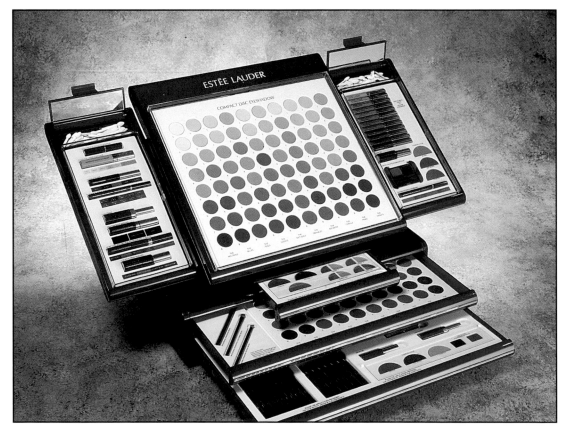

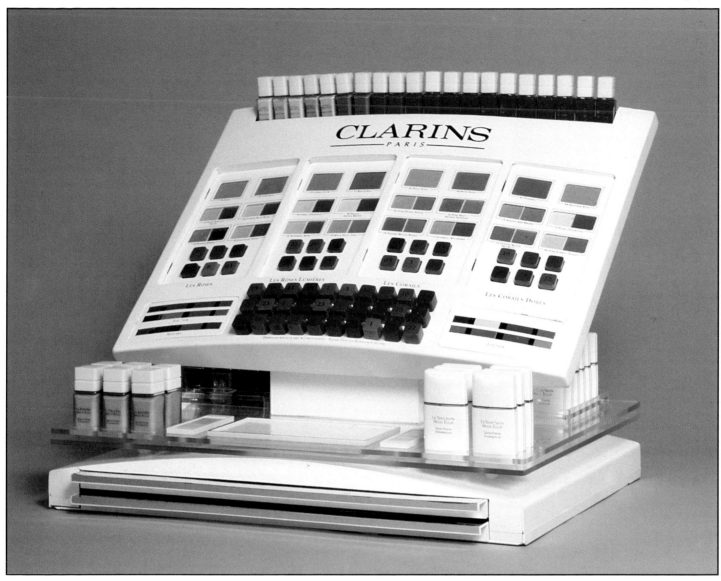

TITLE:

Full Line Colour Display

DIVISION:

Permanent

SUB-CAT:

Multiple Product Line Merchandisers

CLIENT:

Clarins USA, Inc.

ENTRANT:

P.O.P., Inc.
Long Island City, NY

AWARD:

Gold

Injection molding, vacuum forming, hot stamping and metal were utilized by P.O.P., Inc., of Long Island City, NY, to build a display to be used in department and specialty stores by Clarins USA. One thousand four hundred units would be constructed at a cost of $250 to $500 per unit, and could be used for a period of three years.

The display had to attract in-store traffic to Clarins' Full Color Line, had to be more consumer friendly, and be easy to update with new product lines. By using a gloss white with delicate gold trim, the display brings focus to the array of color and attracts the consumer. The display's smaller size, lower height and better angle on the product face sends a consumer friendly message. Removable clear covers, templates and vacuum formed inserts allow consultants to update the display as the product line increases.

TITLE:
Almalfi Spring Line

DIVISION:
Permanent

SUB-CAT:
Testers

CLIENT:
Halston/Borghese, Inc.

ENTRANT:
Dauman Displays, Inc.
New York, NY

AWARD:
Bronze

TITLE:
Elizabeth Arden Military Display Unit

DIVISION:
Permanent

SUB-CAT:
Multiple Product Line Merchandisers

CLIENT:
Elizabeth Arden

ENTRANT:
Dauman Displays, Inc.
New York, NY

AWARD:
Silver

TITLE:

Maybeline "Shades Of You" Pegtalker

DIVISION:

Permanent

SUB-CAT:

Testers

CLIENT:

Maybeline

ENTRANT:

**RTC East,
A Division of RTC Industries
New York, NY**

AWARD:

Silver

TITLE:

Yves Saint Laurent Paris Full Line Display

DIVISION:

Permanent

SUB-CAT:

Multiple Product Line Merchandisers

CLIENT:

Sanofi Beaute, Inc.

ENTRANT:

**The Royal Promotion Group
New York, NY**

AWARD:

Silver

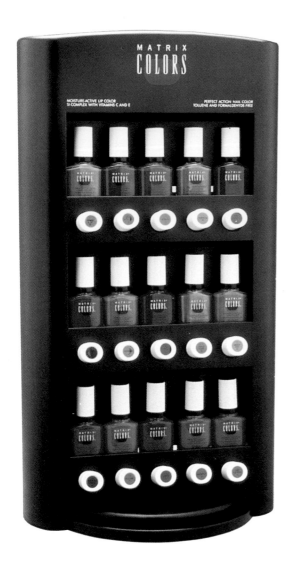

TITLE:
Matrix Essentials Lip & Nail Counter Tester Display

DIVISION:
Permanent

SUB-CAT:
Testers

CLIENT:
Matrix Essentials

ENTRANT:
Thomas A. Schutz Co., Inc.
Morton Grove, IL

AWARD:
Bronze

TITLE:
Elizabeth Arden Master Tester & Pedestal Base

DIVISION:
Permanent

SUB-CAT:
Testers

CLIENT:
Elizabeth Arden

ENTRANT:
Dauman Displays, Inc.
New York, NY

AWARD:
Bronze

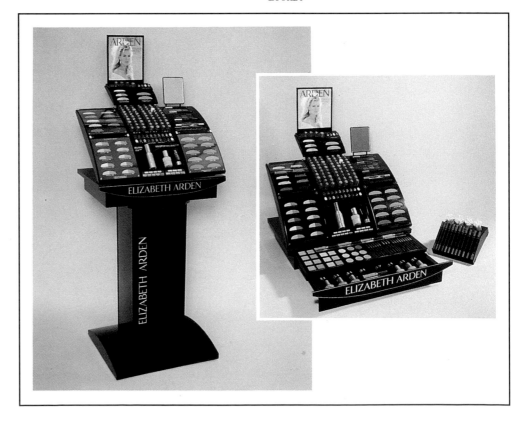

TITLE:

L'Oreal Helping Hands On-Counter Display

DIVISION:

Temporary

SUB-CAT:

Single Product Line Merchandisers

CLIENT:

L'Oreal

ENTRANT:

**Ultimate Display Industries, Inc.
Jamaica, NY**

AWARD:

Bronze

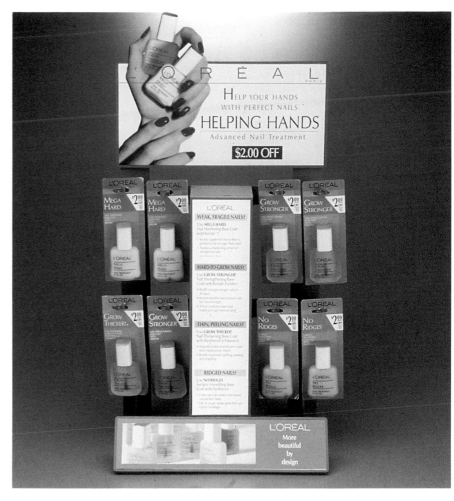

TITLE:

Matrix Essentials Professional Cosmetic Brush Display

DIVISION:

Permanent

SUB-CAT:

Testers

CLIENT:

Matrix Essentials

ENTRANT:

**Thomas A. Schutz Company, Inc.
Morton Grove, IL**

AWARD:

Silver

TITLE:
Lancome Full Line Makeup Center

DIVISION:
Permanent

SUB-CAT:
Multiple Product Line Merchandisers

CLIENT:
Lancome, Inc.

ENTRANT:
**Display Producers, Inc.
Bronx, NY**

AWARD:
Bronze

TITLE:
**Estee Lauder - Compact Disc
Eyeshadow Promotional Unit**

DIVISION:
Permanent

SUB-CAT:
Single Product Line Merchandisers

CLIENT:
Estee Lauder, Inc.

ENTRANT:
**Consumer Promotions, Inc.
Mt. Vernon, NY**

AWARD:
Bronze

TITLE:

Ultima Lip Sexxxy Tower

DIVISION:

Temporary

SUB-CAT:

Single Product Line Merchandisers

CLIENT:

Revlon, Inc.

ENTRANT:

**Advertising Display Co.
Englewood Cliffs, NJ**

AWARD:

Silver

TITLE:

**L'Oreal "So So Rococo" Fall Shade
On-Counter Display**

DIVISION:

Temporary

SUB-CAT:

Testers

CLIENT:

L'Oreal, Inc.

ENTRANT:

**Display Producers, Inc.
Bronx, NY**

AWARD:

Silver

TITLE:

Maybelline "Shades Of You" Spinner

DIVISION:

Temporary

SUB-CAT:

Multiple Product Line Merchandisers

CLIENT:

Maybelline

ENTRANT:

**RTC East,
A Division of RTC Industries
New York, NY**

AWARD:

Silver

TITLE:

Benetton Lip, Nail And Eye

DIVISION:

Permanent

SUB-CAT:

Multiple Product Line Merchandisers

CLIENT:

Benetton Cosmetics Corp.

ENTRANT:

**Advertising Display Co.
Englewood Cliffs, NJ**

AWARD:

Bronze

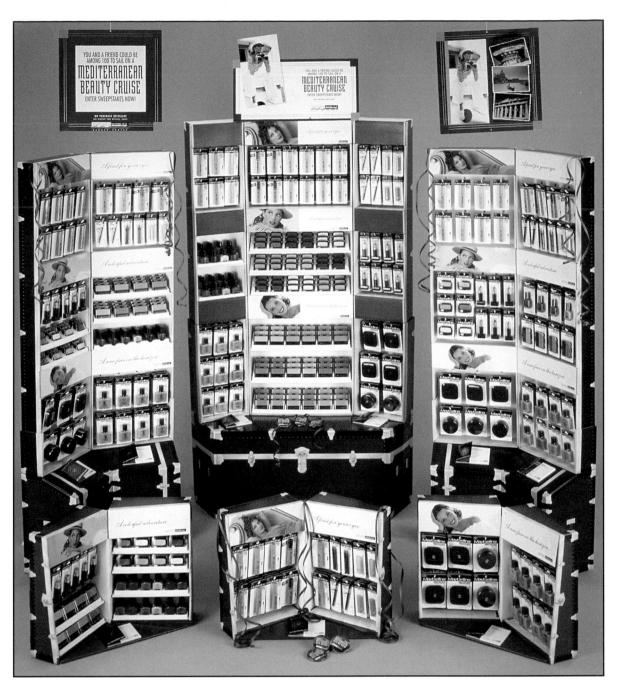

TITLE:

Maybelline Beauty Cruise Sweepstakes

DIVISION:

Temporary

SUB-CAT:

Multiple Product Line Merchandisers

CLIENT:

Maybelline

ENTRANT:

Niven Marketing Group
Elk Grove Village, IL

AWARD:

Gold

The Niven Marketing Group of Elk Grove Village, IL, developed a program for Maybelline that included window banners, danglers, wall mounted signs, and buttons for cosmetitians to wear to promote a Beauty Cruise event. The displays were designed to look like upscale steamer trunks to promote the event. The P-O-P program would be placed in mass-merchan-disers, drug stores, discount merchandisers and specialty outlets.

The displays included three counter and three floor displays. Three sizes of floor displays were constructed to accommodate varying retail floor space. The program was shipped 85 to 95 percent preassembled with product for quick in-store assembly.

The displays feature four color litho mounted corrugated with vacuum formed shelves for uncarded products, and plastic peghooks for carded products. Colorful graphics on the steamer trunk conveyed the beauty and glamour of Maybelline cosmetics along with the Mediterranean Cruise Grand Prize.

Thirty-three thousand counter displays, 2,000 small floor displays, 1,100 large floor displays and 1,050 jumbo floor displays were constructed. The prices to construct ranged from $10 to $15 for the counter displays to $50 to $100 for the jumbo displays. The program was launched in May of 1993, and was in place for one month.

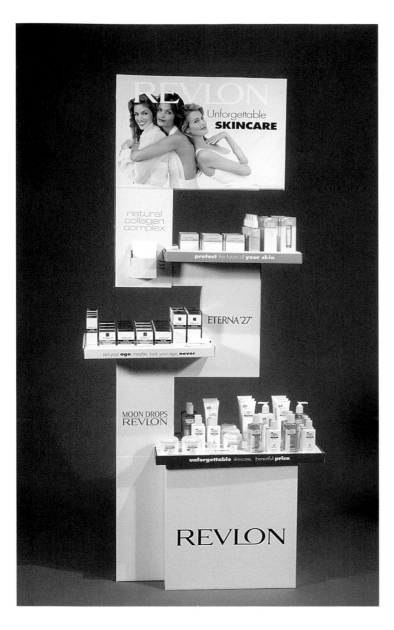

TITLE:
Treatment Floorstand

DIVISION:
Temporary

SUB-CAT:
Multiple Product Line Merchandisers

CLIENT:
Revlon, Inc.

ENTRANT:
**Oxford Innovations,
Tim-Bar Corporation
Hanover, PA**

AWARD:
Silver

TITLE:
Eboné Tester Counter Display

DIVISION:
Temporary

SUB-CAT:
Testers

CLIENT:
Eboné

ENTRANT:
**Acclaim Display & Design Group
Santa Ana, CA**

AWARD:
Bronze

TITLE:

Estee Lauder—Summer Color Story—Blush of Pearls

DIVISION:

Temporary

SUB-CAT:

Multiple Product Line Merchandisers

CLIENT:

Estee Lauder, Inc.

ENTRANT:

P.O.P., Inc.
Long Island City, NY

AWARD:

Bronze

TITLE:

**L'Oreal Colour Riche Hydrating Lip
Colour On-Counter Displays**

DIVISION:

Temporary

SUB CAT:

Single Product Line Merchandisers

CLIENT:

L'Oreal, Inc.

ENTRANT:

Display Producers, Inc.
Bronx, NY

AWARD:

Bronze

TITLE:
Yves Saint Laurent Beaute Outpost

DIVISION:
Permanent

SUB-CAT:
Multiple Product Line Merchandisers

CLIENT:
Sanofi Beaute, Inc.

ENTRANT:
**The Royal Promotion Group
New York, NY**

AWARD:
Bronze

TITLE:
Max Factor International Restage Display Program

DIVISION:
Temporary

SUB-CAT:
Multiple Product Line Merchandisers

CLIENT:
P&G, Cosmetic & Fragrance Products

ENTRANT:
**Henschel-Steinau, Inc.
Englewood, NJ**

AWARD:
Silver

TITLE:
Accentuous Mascara Floorstand (L'Oreal)

DIVISION:
Temporary

SUB-CAT:
Single Product Line Merchandisers

CLIENT:
L'Oreal

ENTRANT:
Ultimate Display Industries, Inc.
Jamaica, NY

AWARD:
Gold

A display was needed to launch L'Oreal's new mascara. The display had to build on the company's previous success and leadership in the mascara market.

Corrugated cardboard, silk screening, wood and a PC chipboard were used to create a floorstand of a large mascara. The display was placed in high traffic areas. It had product on two sides and stimulated purchases and encouraged trial. Originally a three-month run was anticipated for the display, but due to increased selling the display stayed in place longer.

Built by Ultimate Display Industries, Jamaica, NY, it cost between $15 and $25 to build. Two thousand units were produced.

TITLE:
Almay Teen Line Introduction (Treatment and Color)

DIVISION:
Temporary

SUB-CAT:
Multiple Product Line Merchandisers

CLIENT:
Revlon

ENTRANT:
**Ultimate Display Industries, Inc.
Jamaica, NY**

AWARD:
Bronze

TITLE:
Smackers Counter Display

DIVISION:
Temporary

SUB-CAT:
Multiple Product Line Merchandisers

CLIENT:
Bonne Bell

ENTRANT:
**Stone Container Corp.
Richmond, VA**

AWARD:
Silver

TITLE:
Yves Saint Laurent Photographic Lip Banner

DIVISION:
Permanent

SUB-CAT:
Single Product Line Merchandisers

CLIENT:
Sanofi Beaute, Inc.

ENTRANT:
The Royal Promotion Group New York, NY

AWARD:
Bronze

TITLE:
Estee Lauder - Shades Of The Rain Forest

DIVISION:
Temporary

SUB-CAT:
Multiple Product Line Merchandisers

CLIENT:
Estee Lauder, Inc.

ENTRANT:
Consumer Promotions, Inc. Mt. Vernon, NY

AWARD:
Bronze

TITLE:
Mickey The Maestro

DIVISION:
Permanent

SUB-CAT:
Movies, Tapes, Records, CDs

CLIENT:
Walt Disney Records

ENTRANT:
RTC Industries, Inc.
Chicago, IL

AWARD:
Gold

Walt Disney Records needed a display that was accessible to both adults and children, provided a vehicle for short-term promotions of new products or titles, and tie into in-line merchandising. RTC Industries, Chicago, IL, utilized plastic, metal, pegboard, vacuum forming, injection molding, plastic extruding, metal fabrication, powder coating, distortion screening and lithography, to develop 3,000 display to be used over a period of three years. The unit cost between $100 and $250 to build.

Using Mickey Mouse as the focus of the display, the unit had dual-sided merchandising to increase the number of SKUs in the store. The display design allowed it to be placed in other non-traditional place in the store besides the music section. The display was low for easy access and accessible to children. The display allowed flexibility so that it could be used to promote new products and special offers. Changeable graphic header strips accommodate new promotional messages. The display provided a self sufficient platform for the products without requiring plan-o-frame revisions by the retailer.

TITLE:
Apple Power CD Display

DIVISION:
Permanent

SUB-CAT:
Movies, Tapes, Records, CDs

CLIENT:
Apple Computer

ENTRANT:
DCI Marketing
Milwaukee, WI

AWARD:
Silver

TITLE:
Sony Interactive Mini Disc Program

DIVISION:
Permanent

SUB-CAT:
Home Entertainment

CLIENT:
Sony Corp. of America

ENTRANT:
Thomson-Leeds Co., Inc.
New York, NY

AWARD:
Silver

TITLE:
Nintendo Secure Game Pak Browser System

DIVISION:
Permanent

SUB-CAT:
Home Entertainment

CLIENT:
Nintendo of America Inc.

ENTRANT:
Frank Mayer & Associates, Inc. Grafton, WI

AWARD:
Gold

A display was needed that allowed video games to be viewed without the threat of theft due to the small size. The challenge was to develop a display that showcased an entire line of product in a small space, provide security for live product and eliminate out-of-stock problems, offer ease of view for the consumer by accessing the front and back, be maintenance-free and easy to restock, and be adaptable to all types of store environments.

Nintendo of America chose Frank Mayer and Associates of Grafton, WI, to develop the display. Mayer developed a display that consisted of vertical columns that could contain up to eight games. One frame can be hinged from the rear resulting in a high concentration of columns in a narrow space. Live product is contained within a page and is secured behind a molded plexiglass cover. The product is accessed through a keyed, sliding door on the front edge of the page. The display allows several consumers to view games at the same time by utilizing a flip page technique.

The display can be used as a single item or grouped for a larger display. Extra product can be stored in drawer units for easy restocking. Constructed of injection molded plexiglass, formed metal with powdered epoxy coating, stainless spring steel door slide, graphics, illuminated valance, electrical vacuum formed modified styrene, and an injection molded graphic "World of Nintendo" panel.

The display cost over $500 to build and has an intended use of five years. Over 50,000 of the displays were constructed.

TITLE:
Nintendo Interactive Display,
w/Pedestal, For/Super NES

DIVISION:
Permanent

SUB-CAT:
Home Entertainment

CLIENT:
Nintendo Of America Inc.

ENTRANT:
Thomas A. Schutz, Inc.
Pacific Division
Los Angeles, CA

AWARD:
Silver

TITLE:
Just For Kids Castle Display

DIVISION:
Permanent

SUB-CAT:
Movies, Tapes, Records, CDs

CLIENT:
Integrity Music

ENTRANT:
Kin Products
Cincinnati, OH

AWARD:
Bronze

TITLE:
Nintendo M/3I Power Previews Interactive Shelf Display

DIVISION:
Permanent

SUB-CAT:
Home Entertainment

CLIENT:
Nintendo of America Inc.

ENTRANT:
KCS Industries, Inc.,
A Banta Corp. Subsidiary
Milwaukee, WI

AWARD:
Bronze

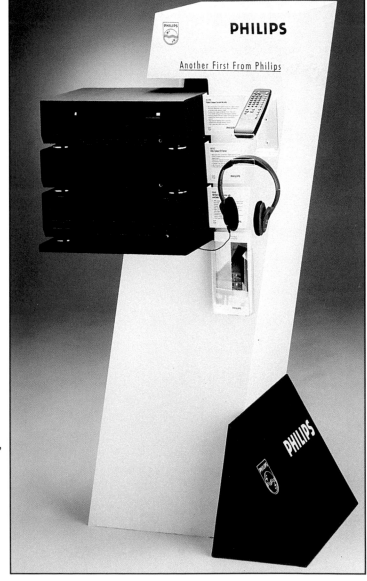

TITLE:
Sony ES/Julliard Literature Display

DIVISION:
Permanent

SUB-CAT:
Home Entertainment

CLIENT:
Sony Corp. of America

ENTRANT:
Display Masters
Long Island City, NY

AWARD:
Silver

TITLE:
Philips DCC 900 Series Selling Station

DIVISION:
Permanent

SUB-CAT:
Home Entertainment - Non-Interactive,
Non-Motion, Non-Illuminated

CLIENT:
Philips Consumer Electronics

ENTRANT:
Display Systems, Inc.
Maspeth, NY

AWARD:
Bronze

TITLE:

Sega Modular Interactive (Generation II) Display

DIVISION:

Permanent

SUB-CAT:

Home Entertainment

CLIENT:

Sega Of America

ENTRANT:

**RTC Industries, Inc.
Chicago, IL**

AWARD:

Bronze

TITLE:

Sega 4' Feature End Cap Display

DIVISION:

Permanent

SUB-CAT:

Home Entertainment

CLIENT:

Sega Of America

ENTRANT:

**RTC Industries, Inc.
Chicago, IL**

AWARD:

Bronze

TITLE:
"Aladdin" Home Video Standee

DIVISION:
Temporary

SUB-CAT:
Movies, Tapes, Records, CDs

CLIENT:
Walt Disney Home Video

ENTRANT:
**Continental Graphics Marketing
Los Angeles, CA**

AWARD:
Gold

To alert the consumers that Walt Disney Home Video was releasing the huge success "Aladdin," a standee was needed to re-create the enhancement and setting of the movie. The standee featured Aladdin, Jasmine and Abu on the flying magic carpet. The display also had to feature tie-ins with two other corporate sponsors.

Continental Graphics Marketing, Los Angeles, CA, constructed a standee using four-color process printed on .024 BSK with parts die-cut to shape. Flexo printed one color on #1 white-one-side corrugated, and silkscreened one color .010 clear acetate, die-cut also was used. Barbettes aid in the assembly of the "Flow-motion" device.

A specially designed dangler system allowed airflow to create the image of flight. The setting for the key image of the display was the representation of the palace and a panoramic effect of the city of Agrabah. The video cassette box was placed in a simple lugin, allowing the price to be customized. The two tie-ins lugins attach to the base, and were designed in a "carpet-like" graphic shape to be thematic. The unit was under 84" and could be shipped via UPS.

There were 26,750 displays manufactured for the campaign at a cost of $10 to $15 to produced. The display was to be used in the retail setting for a four- to six-month period.

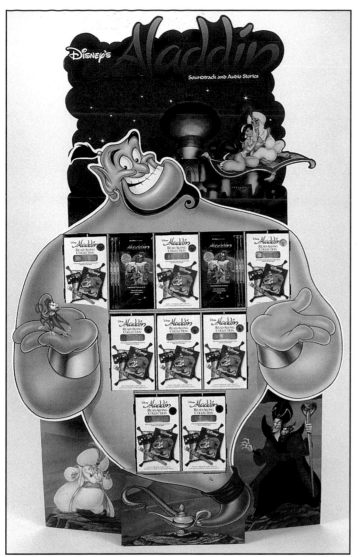

TITLE:
Aladdin Spectacular

DIVISION:
Temporary

SUB-CAT:
Home Entertainment

CLIENT:
Walt Disney Records

ENTRANT:
**Chesapeake Display & Packaging Co.
Winston-Salem, NC**

AWARD:
Bronze

TITLE:
Disney/Pinocchio Floor Display

DIVISION:
Temporary

SUB-CAT:
**Home Entertainment - Non-Interactive,
Non-Motion, Non-Illuminated**

CLIENT:
Buena Vista Home Video

ENTRANT:
**Atlas Display Co.,
A Division of Dyment, Ltd.
Monterey Park, CA**

AWARD:
Silver

TITLE:
Beauty and the Beast - Standee

DIVISION:
Temporary

SUB-CAT:
Movies, Tapes, Records, CDs

CLIENT:
Buena Vista Home Video

ENTRANT:
**Chesapeake Display & Packaging Co.
Winston-Salem, NC**

AWARD:
Silver

TITLE:

Pinocchio Cube

DIVISION:

Temporary

SUB-CAT:

Movies, Tapes, Records, CDs

CLIENT:

The Walt Disney Co.

ENTRANT:

**Jefferson Sumrfit Corp.,
Tri-Pack Division
Toluca Lake, CA**

AWARD:

Silver

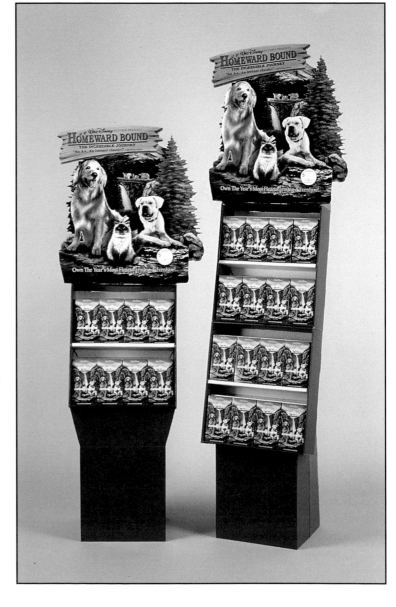

TITLE:

Homeward Bound Universal Prepack

DIVISION:

Temporary

SUB-CAT:

Movies, Tapes, Records, CDs

CLIENT:

The Walt Disney Co.

ENTRANT:

**Jefferson Sumrfit Corp.,
Tri-Pack Division
Toluca Lake, CA**

AWARD:

Silver

TITLE:

Scripture Memory Display

DIVISION:

Permanent

SUB-CAT:

Movies, Tapes, Records, CDs

CLIENT:

Integrity Music

ENTRANT:

**Kin Products
Cincinnati, OH**

AWARD:

Bronze

TITLE:

The Little Engine That Could Merchandiser

DIVISION:

Temporary

SUB-CAT:

Movies, Tapes, Records, CDs

CLIENT:

MCA/Universal Home Video

ENTRANT:

**Great Northern Corp.,
Display Group
Racine, WI**

AWARD:

Gold

A 24-count and 48-count floor display was needed to promote the MCA/Universal Home Video release of "The Little Engine That Could." The display had to use as little floor space as possible, be a self advertiser, and attract children as well as parents. The display had to be easy to assemble at retail.

Using flexographic printed B-flute corrugated and hand gluing the display held 96 videos while resembling the little engine. Tilt back angles of the product was built into the trays and kept the footprint to a minimum. The trays were pre-assembled and packed with product to make set-up easy at retail.

The displays was constructed by Great Northern Corp., Racine, WI, and 550 units were constructed. The display was intended for six to eight weeks of use at a cost of $25 to $50 per display and was placed in Target, K-Mart, Toys-R-Us, Blockbuster, Camelot and Transworld stores.

TITLE:
Car Songs

DIVISION:
Temporary

SUB-CAT:
Movies, Tapes, Records, CDs

CLIENT:
Western Publishing Co.

ENTRANT:
**Stone Container Corp.
Richmond, VA**

AWARD:
Bronze

TITLE:
Golden Book Video Classic Display

DIVISION:
Temporary

SUB-CAT:
Movies, Tapes, Recoords, CDs

CLIENT:
Western Publishing Co., Inc

ENTRANT:
**Great Northern Corp.,
Display Group
Racine, WI**

AWARD:
Bronze

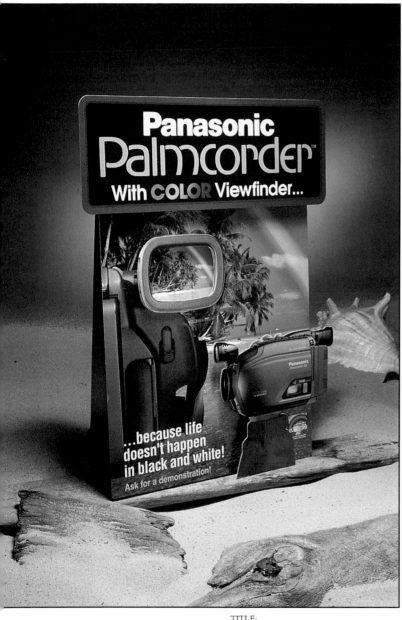

TITLE:
Leap Of Faith Standee

DIVISION:
Temporary

SUB-CAT:
Movies, Tapes, Records, CDs

CLIENT:
Paramount Home Video

ENTRANT:
**Paramount Home Video
Hollywood, CA**

AWARD:
Bronze

TITLE:
Panasonic Palmcorder Viewfinder

DIVISION:
Temporary

SUB-CAT:
Home Entertainment

CLIENT:
Panasonic

ENTRANT:
**Frank Mayer & Associates, Inc.
Grafton, WI**

AWARD:
Bronze

TITLE:

Giorgio Beverly Hills "Wings Deluxe And Single Tester"

DIVISION:

Permanent

SUB-CAT:

Women's Perfumes

CLIENT:

Giorgio Beverly Hills

ENTRANT:

**Consumer Promotions, Inc.
Mt. Vernon, NY**

AWARD:

Gold

Giorgio Beverly Hills required a display that was innovative, durable and affordable. The display had to stand out among other counter displays and glorify the product in retail environments.

The display created high visibility impact and captivated consumer attention by using a faux granite base, a custom fabricated product retainer, a two-piece injection molded riser panel, a hand cast color matched resin ball and a gold briched incised logo.

Consumer Promotions, Inc., of Mt. Vernon, NY, constructed the display to be used for a two-year time period. At a cost of $50 to $100 to construct, 1,500 deluxe units and 1,450 single units were constructed.

TITLE:
Estee Lauder Fragrance/Lotion Tester

DIVISION:
Permanent

SUB-CAT:
Men's and Women's Colognes, Fragrances, Eau de Toilette, etc.

CLIENT:
Estee Lauder Corp.

ENTRANT:
**Trans World Marketing
East Rutherford, NJ**

AWARD:
Silver

TITLE:
Clarins Elysium Tester Display

DIVISION:
Permanent

SUB-CAT:
Women's Perfumes

CLIENT:
Clarins USA

ENTRANT:
**Shannen Promotions, Inc.
New York, NY**

AWARD:
Silver

TITLE:
Minotaure Outpost

DIVISION:
Permanent

SUB-CAT:
Men's and Women's Colognes, Fragrances, Eau de Toilette, etc.

CLIENT:
Cosmair, Inc.

ENTRANT:
**The Royal Promotion Group
New York, NY**

AWARD:
Bronze

TITLE:
Gio de Giorgio Armani Outpost

DIVISION:
Permanent

SUB-CAT:
Women's Perfumes

CLIENT:
Cosmair, Inc.

ENTRANT:
**The Royal Promotion Group
New York, NY**

AWARD:
Silver

TITLE:

Muehlens Tres Jourdan

DIVISION:

Permanent

SUB-CAT:

Women's Perfumes

CLIENT:

Muehlens

ENTRANT:

**Advertising Display Co.
Englewood Cliffs, NJ**

AWARD:

Gold

Advertising Display Co., Englewood Cliffs, NJ, had to create a display for a launch tester vehicle that would enhance the upscale packaging and convey the quality image of Charles Jourdan. Five hundred units were created to be used for a period of up to one year.

A frost plexiglass created a diffused light on the fragrance when in position. A subliminal association was also transmitted with high-heeled Jourdan shoes with the display. Acrylic fabrication and silk screening were used in the display that was successful in portraying the upscale nature of the product. The cost per unit was $50 to $100.

TITLE:

Stetson Floorstand

DIVISION:

Temporary

SUB-CAT:

Men's and Women's Colognes, Fragrances, Eau de Toilette, etc.

CLIENT:

Coty, Inc.

ENTRANT:

**Trans World Marketing
East Rutherford, NJ**

AWARD:

Bronze

TITLE:

Chanel 3 Panel Tabletop Screen and Printed Bags

DIVISION:

Permanent

SUB-CAT:

Women's Perfumes

CLIENT:

Chanel, Inc.

ENTRANT:

**Shannen Promotions, Inc.
New York, NY**

AWARD:

Bronze

TITLE:

Cosmair - Minotaure Deluxe Tester/Mini Tester

DIVISION:

Permanent

SUB-CAT:

Men's and Women's Colognes, Fragrances, Eau de Toilette, etc.

CLIENT:

Cosmair, Inc.

ENTRANT:

**Consumer Promotions, Inc.
Mt. Vernon, NY**

AWARD:

Bronze

TITLE:

Naf Naf Spring Feed Shelving System

DIVISION:

Permanent

SUB-CAT:

Women's Perfumes

CLIENT:

Gemey - Paris

ENTRANT:

**Dauman Displays, Inc.
New York, NY**

AWARD:

Silver

TITLE:
Chaps Ralph Lauren Maritime Collection Prepack

DIVISION:
Temporary

SUB-CAT:
Men's and Women's Colognes, Fragrances, Eau de Toilette, etc.

CLIENT:
L'Oreal, Inc.

ENTRANT:
**Display Producers, Inc.
Bronx, NY**

AWARD:
Silver

TITLE:
Gio de Giorgio Armani Modular Counter

DIVISION:
Permanent

SUB-CAT:
Women's Perfumes

CLIENT:
Cosmair, Inc.

ENTRANT:
**The Royal Promotion Group
New York, NY**

AWARD:
Bronze

TITLE:

Coty L'Effleur Gift Shoppe

DIVISION:

Temporary

SUB-CAT:

Men's and Women's Colognes, Fragrances, Eau de Toilette, etc.

CLIENT:

Coty, Inc.

ENTRANT:

**Trans World Marketing
East Rutherford, NJ**

AWARD:

Gold

A display to be used in chain drug stores and mass merchandisers was needed by Coty, Inc., to encourage consumers to purchase Coty L'Effluer as the gift for Mother's Day. Trans World Marketing, East Rutherford, NJ, created a display that allowed retailers to create a customized "mini-boutique" for the line.

The display featured soft tones to create a cozy environment for the product. The sides of the unit replicate window panes that allowed consumers to fully view the product and experience the product's aroma. The display had injection-molded sides and header, and a corrugated shelf.

The display cost between $5 and $10 and could be used for up to six weeks. Eighteen thousand units were built.

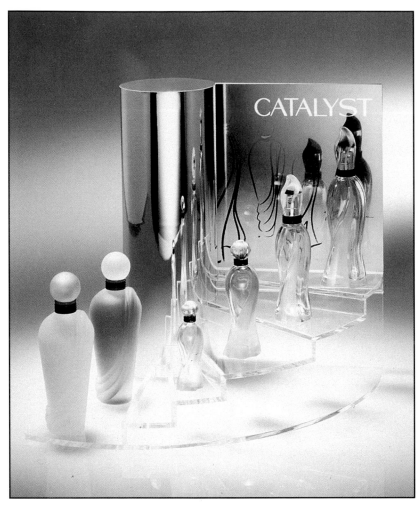

TITLE:
Halston Catalyst Staircase

DIVISION:
Permanent

SUB-CAT:
Women's Perfumes

CLIENT:
Halston/Borghese, Inc.

ENTRANT:
Dauman Displays, Inc.
New York, NY

AWARD:
Bronze

TITLE:
Tribu Fragrance Launch Display

DIVISION:
Temporary

SUB-CAT:
Men's and Women's Colognes, Fragrances,
Eau de Toilette, etc.

CLIENT:
Benetton Cosmetics Corp.

ENTRANT:
Advertising Display Co.
Englewood Cliffs, NJ

AWARD:
Bronze

TITLE:

Coty Vanilla Fields Launch

DIVISION:

Temporary

SUB-CAT:

Men's and Women's Colognes, Fragrances, Eau de Toilette, etc.

CLIENT:

Coty, Inc.

ENTRANT:

**Trans World Marketing
East Rutherford, NJ**

AWARD:

Silver

TITLE:

Ralph Lauren Chaps' Christmas On-Counter Display

DIVISION:

Temporary

SUB-CAT:

Men's and Women's Colognes, Fragrances, Eau de Toilette, etc.

CLIENT:

L'Oreal

ENTRANT:

**L'Oreal
New York, NY**

AWARD:

Bronze

TITLE:
The Original Brewnut

DIVISION:
Permanent

SUB-CAT:
Containerized and Processed Foods

CLIENT:
Loretta Foods

ENTRANT:
Graphic Workshop Studios, Ltd.
Mississauga, ONT, Canada

AWARD:
Gold

The display was to be placed in national supermarkets chains and smaller independent grocery stores, specifically in an aisle. The display had to entice customers to try the product, promote the product as a high-end snack, and aggressively catch the consumer's attention.

A four-color large photo depicting the product would show the honey color and coating on the peanut. The design of the product's label made it appear as a premium product. A photograph of an oversized bottle made the display eye catching, and by stacking cartons of products to eye level made them visible to customers.

Constructed by Graphics Workshop Studios, Ltd., Mississauga, ONT, Canada for Loretta Foods, the display utilized corrugated cardboard coated on two sides. The display was to be used for a one-year time period and 2,000 units were constructed. The cost was $10 to $15 per unit.

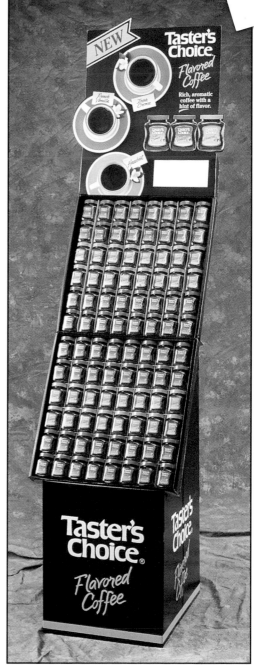

TITLE:

A-1 Steak Sauce Case Stacker

DIVISION:

Temporary

SUB-CAT:

Containerized and Processed Foods

CLIENT:

Nabisco Foods

ENTRANT:

Al Gar/The Display Connection, Inc.
Clifton, NJ

AWARD:

Bronze

TITLE:

Airwaves 72 Pc. Refill Sidekick/Floorstand

DIVISION:

Temporary

SUB-CAT:

Paper Goods and Soap

CLIENT:

Reckitt & Colman, Inc.

ENTRANT:

JSC/Tri-Pack,
Jefferson Smurfit Corp.
Carlstadt, NJ

AWARD:

Silver

TITLE:

Nestle Tasters Choice Flavored Coffee
Trial Size Shipper

DIVISION:

Temporary

SUB-CAT:

Containerized and Processed Foods

CLIENT:

Nestle Beverage Co.

ENTRANT:

HML Designs, Inc.
Coral Springs, FL

AWARD:

Bronze

TITLE:
A-1 Floor Display

DIVISION:
Temporary

SUB-CAT:
Containerized and Processed Foods

CLIENT:
Planters Lifesavers Co.

ENTRANT:
Decision Point Marketing
Winston-Salem, NC

AWARD:
Silver

TITLE:
Wardley Ten

DIVISION:
Temporary

SUB-CAT:
Pet Food and Accessories

CLIENT:
Wardley Corp.

ENTRANT:
McLean Packaging Corp.
Philadelphia, PA

AWARD:
Bronze

McCormick wanted a display that was inexpensive, versatile and attention getting for its ground pepper. It also had to accommodate a variety of product sizes and be shipped flat. The display, constructed of corrugated cardboard, was built by Display Masters, Long Island City, NY. Five thousand units were made to be used for a two- to three-week period. It cost under $5 to build.

The display drew attention to the readily identifiable McCormick pepper. It was versatile in displaying different sizes of product, and was easily packed and assembled.

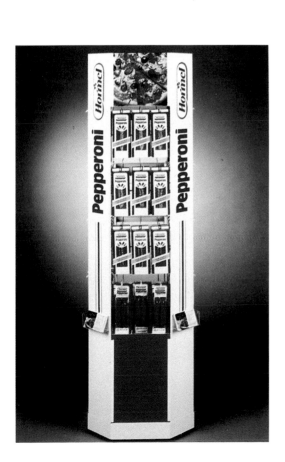

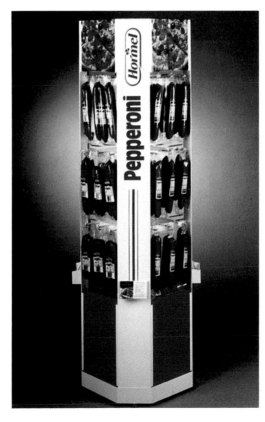

TITLE:
McCormick Pepper Dump Display

DIVISION:
Temporary

SUB-CAT:
Containerized and Processed Foods

CLIENT:
McCormick

ENTRANT:
Display Masters
Long Island City, NY

AWARD:
Gold

TITLE:
Hormel Pepperoni Profit Tower

DIVISION:
Permanent

SUB-CAT:
Containerized and Processed Foods

CLIENT:
Hormel Foods Corp.

ENTRANT:
Advertising Display Co.
Englewood Cliffs, NJ

AWARD:
Silver

TITLE:

Kraft Cheese Center

DIVISION:

Permanent

SUB-CAT:

Containerized and Processed Foods

CLIENT:

Kraft General Foods

ENTRANT:

**Henschel-Steinau, Inc.
Englewood, NJ**

AWARD:

Bronze

TITLE:

Tetra Consumer Information Center

DIVISION:

Permanent

SUB-CAT:

Pet Food and Accessories

CLIENT:

Tetra Sales USA

ENTRANT:

**Goldring Display Group, Inc.
Paramus, NJ**

AWARD:

Silver

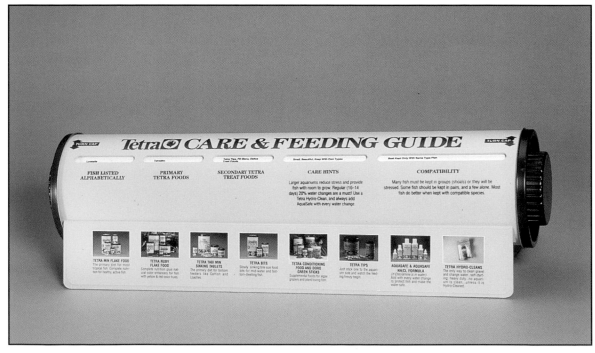

TITLE:
Old El Paso Fun Casa

DIVISION:
Temporary

SUB-CAT:
Containerized and Processed Foods

CLIENT:
Pet Inc.

ENTRANT:
**Henschel-Steinau, Inc.
Englewood, NJ**

AWARD:
Gold

TITLE:
Wonder Tortilla Softwrap Display

DIVISION:
Temporary

SUB-CAT:
Frozen, Fresh and Refrigerated Foods

CLIENT:
Continental Baking Co.

ENTRANT:
**Packaging Corp. of America
Ashland, OH**

AWARD:
Silver

A retail island that could merchandise a large volume of Old El Paso product was needed for use during special promotional events. Events included Cinco DeMayo, July 4th, Mexican Independence Day and the Super Bowl. The display had to create product excitement and brand recognition.

Henschel-Steinau, Inc., Englewood, NJ, created a display utilizing rubber plate printing and die cutting of 200 pound flute with one-sided corrugated, glued and stitched. Injection molded polypropylene fasteners and 20 pound bond paper printed on one side also was used. Two thousand five hundred units were made to be used for a three-week time period. It cost between $15 and $25 to make.

A large two-sided adobe arch was designed out of corrugated to hold a large volume of product. Product could be stacked between the towers or around them. The large billboard-like "Old El Paso" arch section is an integral part of the structure and creates brand awareness. The height, width and depth of the unit was kept to within acceptable limits of retailers.

Assembly was eased at retail by having some components pre-assembled at the factory. The new display took 75 percent less time to assembled compared to past Old El Paso displays. Because of the success of the program Pet, Inc., decided to utilize the display during promotional periods for the next five years.

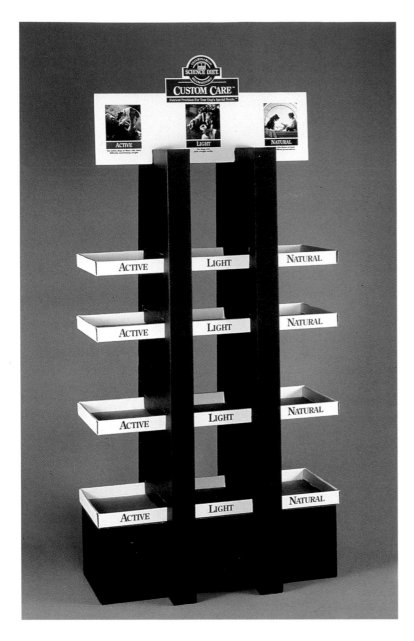

TITLE:
K&L/Hill's Custom Care 4-Way Shoppable Floorstand

DIVISION:
Temporary

SUB-CAT:
Pet Food and Accessories

CLIENT:
K&L Partners

ENTRANT:
**Advertising Display
Englewood Cliffs, NJ**

AWARD:
Silver

TITLE:
Baker's Bunny Floorstand

DIVISION:
Temporary

SUB-CAT:
Containerized and Processed Foods

CLIENT:
Kraft General Foods, Inc.

ENTRANT:
**Rand Display, Inc.
Englewood Cliffs, NJ**

AWARD:
Bronze

TITLE:
Nestle Quik Syrup Prepack Shipper

DIVISION:
Temporary

SUB-CAT:
Containerized and Processed Foods

CLIENT:
Nestle Beverage Co.

ENTRANT:
**HML Designs, Inc.
Coral Springs, FL**

AWARD:
Bronze

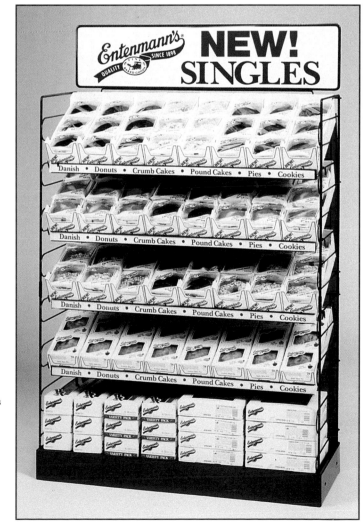

TITLE:
Entenmann's "Singles" Display

DIVISION:
Permanent

SUB-CAT:
Frozen, Fresh and Refrigerated Foods

CLIENT:
Entenmann's, Incorporated

ENTRANT:
**Cannon Equipment Co.
Cannon Falls, MN**

AWARD:
Bronze

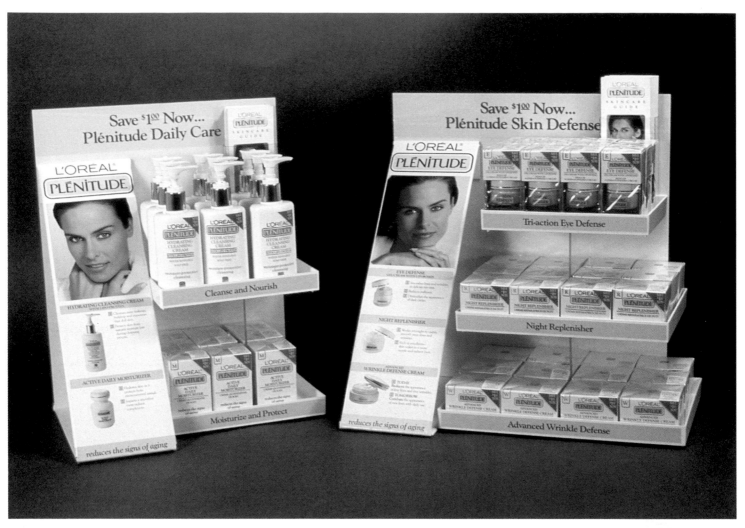

TITLE:
Best Sellers On-Counter Display (Plenitude)

DIVISION:
Permanent

SUB-CAT:
Suntan Products, Lotions, Moisturizers

CLIENT:
L'Oreal

ENTRANT:
Ultimate Display Industries, Inc
Jamaica, NY

AWARD:
Gold

L'Oreal's Plenitude Best Seller display has to promote the best in the treatment and daily care of skin product in a self service environment. A $1 instant coupon also would have to be incorporated into the display.

The display was able to feature the three treatment best sellers and two daily care best sellers. It maximized counter space during peak periods and instructional graphic panels and on pack IRC's encouraged multiple purchases.

Ultimate Display Industries, Inc., Jamaica, NY, utilized injection molded styrene, lithography, corrugated fabricated acrylic and fabricated styrene to construct the display. It cost between $10 and $15 to construct and was to be used for six months. Eight thousand units were constructed.

TITLE:
Glints Counter Display

DIVISION:
Permanent

SUB-CAT:
Hair Styling and Coloring Products

CLIENT:
Clairol, Inc.

ENTRANT:
Henschel-Steinau, Inc.
Englewood, NJ

AWARD:
Silver

TITLE:
Lancome—Full Line Treatment Display

DIVISION:
Permanent

SUB-CAT:
Skin Care

CLIENT:
Lancome, Inc.

ENTRANT:
P.O.P., Inc.
Long Island City, NY

AWARD:
Bronze

TITLE:

Yardley Bath Shoppe Floorstand & Shelf Management System

DIVISION:

Permanent

SUB-CAT:

Suntan Products, Lotions, Moisturizers

CLIENT:

Maybelline, Inc.

ENTRANT:

Display Systems, Inc.
Maspeth, NY

AWARD:

Silver

TITLE:

Joico Large Salon Display

DIVISION:

Permanent

SUB-CAT:

Hair Cleansing Treatment

CLIENT:

Joico Laboratories

ENTRANT:

RTC Industries, Inc.
Chicago, IL

AWARD:

Bronze

Neutrogena Corp. wanted a permanent off-shelf display for the expanding Neutrogena Rainbath Shower Care line in drug stores and mass merchandisers. They wanted to create sales in full-size personal purchases, trial samples and gift giving. The display had to sell from the side and front; provide space for line expansion; and be free standing.

Henschel-Steinau, Inc., Englewood, NJ, created a display that looked like a shower including a facsimile representing a spray of water and fixtures that included a metal shower rod. The display housed 12 dozen full-size products, as well as 96 pieces of 1 ounce samples and 18 saleable gift bags. An optional backwall extender allows for conversion to encap placement, as well as in-aisle placement without the extender. Ease of set-up was accomplished by pre-assembly at the factory.

The display was constructed by using wood, flakeboard, injection molded and vacuum-formed plastic, powder coated wire, plated steel tubing, silk screened logo on vinyl laminate, and hot-stamped corporate I.D. on plastic. The display was designed to be used for a one-year period at a cost of $250 to $500 per unit.

TITLE:
Neutrogena Rainbath Floor Display

DIVISION:
Permanent

SUB-CAT:
Skin Care

CLIENT:
Neutrogena Corp.

ENTRANT:
Henschel-Steinau, Inc.
Englewood, NJ

AWARD:
Gold

TITLE:
Matrix Biolage Body Counter Display

DIVISION:
Permanent

SUB-CAT:
Skin Care

CLIENT:
Matrix Essentials

ENTRANT:
**Thomas A. Schutz Co., Inc.
Morton Grove, IL**

AWARD:
Silver

TITLE:
Estee Lauder - Skin Care Unit

DIVISION:
Permanent

SUB-CAT:
Skin Care

CLIENT:
Estee Lauder, Inc.

ENTRANT:
**Consumer Promotions, Inc.
Mt. Vernon, NY**

AWARD:
Bronze

TITLE:

Marcella Borghese Treatment Center

DIVISION:

Permanent

SUB-CAT:

Skin Care

CLIENT:

Halston/Borghese

ENTRANT:

**Dauman Displays
New York, NY**

AWARD:

Silver

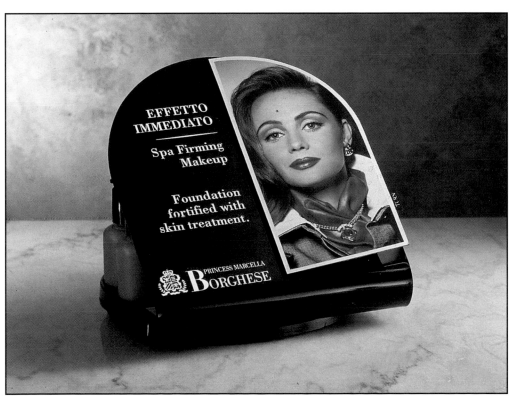

TITLE:

**Princess Marcella Borghese Effetto Immediato
Spa Firming Makeup**

DIVISION:

Permanent

SUB-CAT:

Suntan Products, Lotions, Moisturizers

CLIENT:

Halston/Borghese

ENTRANT:

**Dauman Displays, Inc.
New York, NY**

AWARD:

Bronze

Revlon's display program goal was to introduce and support the launch of the company's newest line of shampoos and conditioners in mass retailers. Two displays were needed, one for the 15-ounce business size and another for a special trial size. Both displays would be prepacked to ease set up at retail.

The floorstand used color and graphics to convey the product's image of glamour and sophistication. A lithographed curved shape of company spokeswomen Claudia Schiffer and Cindy Crawford were featured. Vacuum-formed product trays with wire supports and corrugated display bases completed the unit.

Built by Advertising Display Co., Englewood Cliffs, NJ, the display was to be used for a six- to eight-week period. Five thousand regular size and 2,500 trial size units were constructed. The cost was $10 to $15 per unit to construct.

TITLE:
Outrageous Regular Business And Trial Size Floor Stand

DIVISION:
Temporary

SUB-CAT:
Hair Cleansing Treatment

CLIENT:
Revlon

ENTRANT:
Advertising Display Co. Englewood Cliffs, NJ

AWARD:
Gold

TITLE:
Loving Care: Natural Shades Counter Display

DIVISION:
Temporary

SUB-CAT:
Hair Styling and Coloring Products

CLIENT:
Clairol, Inc.

ENTRANT:
R.E.A. Display, Inc.
Fairfield, NJ

AWARD:
Bronze

TITLE:
Overnight Floorstand (Plenitude Advanced Overnight Replenisher)

DIVISION:
Temporary

SUB-CAT:
Suntan Products, Lotions, Moisturizers

CLIENT:
L'Oreal

ENTRANT:
Ultimate Display Industries, Inc.
Jamaica, NY

AWARD:
Silver

TITLE:
Gillette Cool Wave Series Floorstand

DIVISION:
Temporary

SUB-CAT:
Skin Care

CLIENT:
The Gillette Co.

ENTRANT:
**Advertising Display Co.
Englewood Cliffs, NJ**

AWARD:
Bronze

TITLE:
Oil Of Olay Etagere

DIVISION:
Temporary

SUB-CAT:
Skin Care

CLIENT:
Procter & Gamble Co.

ENTRANT:
**Rand Display, Inc.
Englewood Cliffs, NJ**

AWARD:
Bronze

TITLE:
Head & Shoulders Interactive Shelf Merchandiser

DIVISION:
Temporary

SUB-CAT:
Hair Cleansing Treatment

CLIENT:
The Procter & Gamble Co.

ENTRANT:
**Markson Rosenthal & Co.
Englewood Cliffs, NJ**

AWARD:
Gold

The display had to heighten brand awareness and visibility during the six month introduction of Procter and Gamble's Head & Shoulder new and improved hair care line. It also had to provide the consumer with information to choose the right product for their particular condition, and be flexible enough to merchandise a range of product.

A three-sided panel design challenged the consumer to learn more about the product. The display has a rotating shelf merchandiser in place and a sliding indicator button to move to panel two or three, that recommends the correct product. The panels include

information on scalp conditions, product available and a toll-free number for additional information, and then automatically returns to panel one for the next customer. The spinner in attached by "C" clamps to the shelf where the product is located.

Six thousands of the shelf spinner were created by Markson Rosenthal and Company, Englewood Cliffs, NJ. An extruded center section, injection molded side panels and brackets, lithography laminated four-color process labels and metal "C" clamps were used in the construction. At cost of $5 to $10 per spinner, it was to be used for a six- to 12-month period.

TITLE:

Clarion Skin Care Tray System

DIVISION:

Permanent

SUB-CAT:

Skin Care

CLIENT:

Noxell Corp.

ENTRANT:

Thomson-Leeds Co., Inc.
New York, NY

AWARD:

Bronze

TITLE:

Pantene Pro-V 13oz. Shampoo with
1 oz. On-Pack Floorstand

DIVISION:

Temporary

SUB-CAT:

Hair Cleansing Treatment

CLIENT:

The Procter & Gamble Co.

ENTRANT:

Chesapeake Display & Packaging Co.
Winston-Salem, NC

AWARD:

Bronze

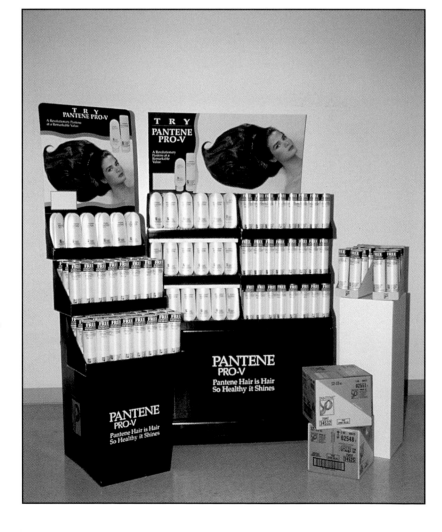

TITLE:

Chap Stick Profit Chute

DIVISION:

Temporary

SUB-CAT:

Skin Care

CLIENT:

A.H. Robins

ENTRANT:

**Henschel-Steinau, Inc.
Englewood, NJ**

AWARD:

Bronze

TITLE:

Gillette Canada Sensor For Women Floor Display

DIVISION:

Temporary

SUB-CAT:

Brushes, Hairdryers, Razors and Combs

CLIENT:

The Gillette Co.

ENTRANT:

**Henschel-Steinau, Inc.
Englewood, NJ**

AWARD:

Silver

TITLE:

Glints Floor Display

DIVISION:

Temporary

SUB-CAT:

Hair Styling and Coloring Products

CLIENT:

Clairol, Inc.

ENTRANT:

**Henschel-Steinau, Inc.
Englewood, NJ**

AWARD:

Silver

TITLE:

Beauty Blitz Floorstand

DIVISION:

Temporary

SUB-CAT:

Brushes, Hairdryers, Razors and Combs

CLIENT:

Paris Presents

ENTRANT:

**Great Northern Corp.,
Display Group
Racine, WI**

AWARD:

Silver

TITLE:

Pierre Fabre Klorane Counter Merchandiser

DIVISION:

Temporary

SUB-CAT:

Hair Cleansing Treatment

CLIENT:

Pierre Fabre

ENTRANT:

**Dauman Displays, Inc.
New York, NY**

AWARD:

Bronze

TITLE:

Pantene Pro-V Shelf Merchandiser

DIVISION.

Temporary

SUB-CAT:

Hair Cleansing Treatment

CLIENT:

The Procter and Gamble Co.

ENTRANT:

**Markson Rosenthal & Co.
Englewood Cliffs, NJ**

AWARD:

Bronze

PERMANENT DISPLAY OF THE YEAR

A display was needed that could accommodate various sizes of Tylenol product, fit into a unique store location, reduce consumer confusion via a symptom analyzer and provide reliable health information through a booklet supplied at the display. McNeil Consumer Products had Mechtronics Corp., Stamford, CT, build a display that was a four-sided floor stand in-line gondola. It would be placed in mass merchandisers.

Key elements of the display included the "Tylenol Store" theme, symptom analyzer and the health information brochure. The display could be used as a two-, three-, or four-sided merchandiser to satisfy each class of trader space requirements. Any module of the display can accept a pre-packed corrugated promotional insert. Molded trays can be stored in the base of the unit.

One thousand of the injection molded styrene, vinyl clad flake board displays were constructed. At a cost of $100 to $250 to construct, the display was intended for a use of two years.

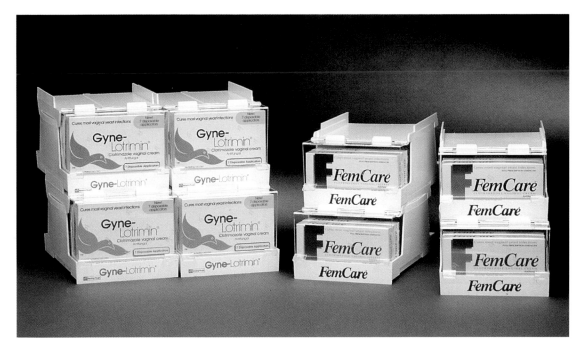

TITLE:
Feminine Products Pilfer-Proof Trays

DIVISION:
Permanent

SUB-CAT:
First Aid and Pharmaceuticals

CLIENT:
Schering-Plough Healthcare Products

ENTRANT:
Trans World Marketing
East Rutherford, NJ

AWARD:
Silver

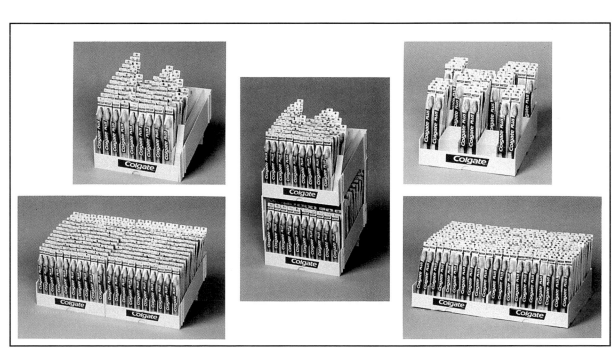

TITLE:
Colgate Toothbrushes On-Shelf Merchandising System

DIVISION:
Permanent

SUB-CAT:
Dentifrices, Mouthwash and Oral Implements

CLIENT:
Colgate-Palmolive Co.

ENTRANT:
Goldring Display Group, Inc.
Paramus, NJ

AWARD:
Bronze

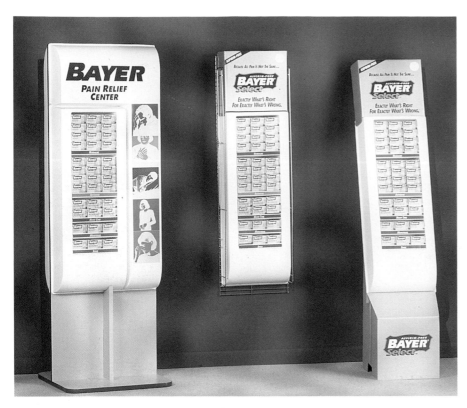

TITLE:
Bayer Select Pre-Pack Merchandising Program

DIVISION:
Temporary

SUB-CAT:
First Aid and Pharmaceuticals

CLIENT:
Sterling Health

ENTRANT:
Consumer Promotions, Inc.
Mt. Vernon, NY

AWARD:
Gold

The display was needed to distinguish Sterling Health's Bayer Select from competing product and differentiate the five symptom specific products within the line. The display would be place in food, mass merchandiser and drug stores.

Consumer Promotion, Inc., of Mt. Vernon, NY, constructed a display of .080 matte styrene trays with extruded shelves, corrugated head and base. The Pain Relief Center constructed of 3/4" particle board to "L" shaped vacuum form attachment. The display consisted of floor stand, sidekick and free-standing product tray that can be individually combined for a variety of account and brand needs. System specific product messages were conveyed through the use of colors and symptom specific text. Icons also were displayed to further communicated the symptom specific pain relief message.

The intended length of use for the display was four to eight weeks. The floorstand and sidekick cost between $25 and $50 to construct and between $100 and $250 for the Pain Relief Center. Two thousand four hundred Pain Relief Centers and 31,000 trays were constructed.

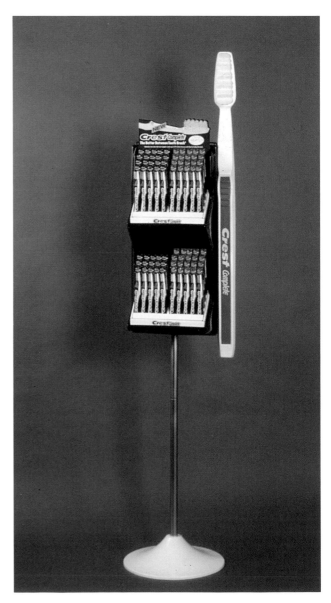

TITLE:
Stomach Care Center Permanent Power Wing

DIVISION:
Permanent

SUB-CAT:
First Aid and Pharmaceuticals

CLIENT:
McNeil Consumer Products Co.

ENTRANT:
Henschel-Steinau, Inc.
Englewood, NJ

AWARD:
Bronze

TITLE:
Crest Complete Spectacular Floorstand

DIVISION:
Temporary

SUB-CAT:
Dentifrices, Mouthwash and Oral Implements

CLIENT:
Procter & Gamble Co.

ENTRANT:
Rand Display, Inc.
Englewood Cliffs, NJ

AWARD:
Bronze

TITLE:
Secret/Sure/Old Spice Summer Deodorant Center

DIVISION:
Temporary

SUB-CAT:
Personal Hygiene, Diapers and Baby Items

CLIENT:
Procter & Gamble Co.

ENTRANT:
Rand Display, Inc.
Englewood Cliffs, NJ

AWARD:
Bronze

TITLE:

Centrum Jr. Shamu Floorstand

DIVISION:

Temporary

SUB-CAT:

First Aid and Pharmaceuticals

CLIENT:

American Cyanamid Co.

ENTRANT:

**Markson Rosenthal and Co.
Englewood Cliffs, NJ**

AWARD:

Bronze

TITLE:

**Visine Bonus Pack Power Wing
Floor Display**

DIVISION:

Temporary

SUB-CAT:

First Aid and Pharmaceuticals

CLIENT:

Pfizer, Inc.

ENTRANT:

**Henschel-Steinau, Inc.
Englewood, NJ**

AWARD:

Bronze

TITLE:

**Duration 1/2 oz. - 24 pc. Floor
Stand/Power Wing**

DIVISION:

Temporary

SUB-CAT:

First Aid and Pharmaceuticals

CLIENT:

Schering-Plough

ENTRANT:

**Packaging Corp. of America,
Trexlertown Container Plant
Lancaster, PA**

AWARD:

Silver

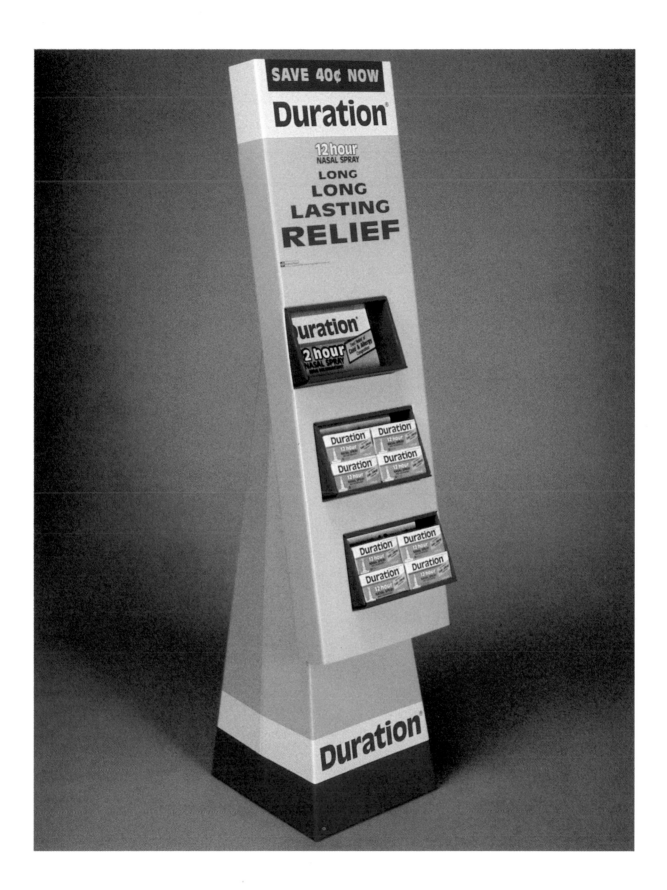

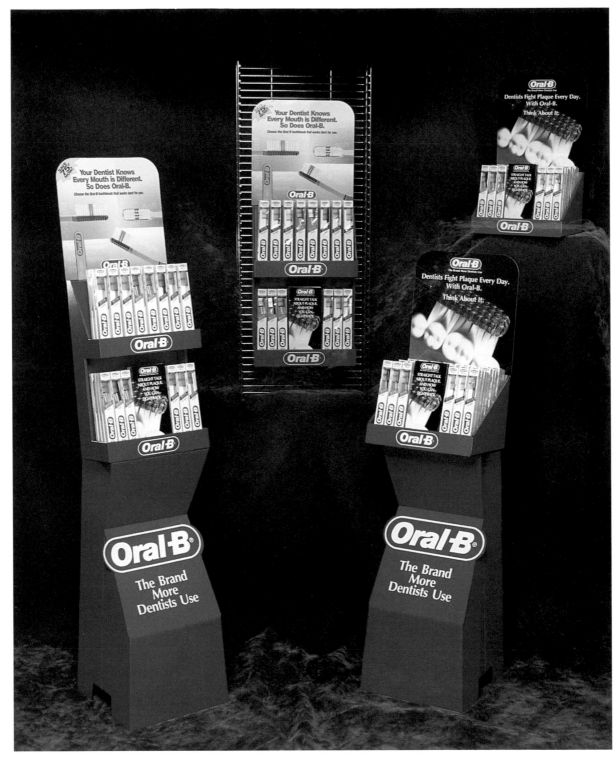

The display program was designed to be used in national and regional drug, food and mass merchandiser stores for a period of four to six weeks. Ten thousand of the displays were manufactured. Chesapeake Display & Packaging, Winston-Salem, NC, constructed the display of vacuum formed trays, flexo printed corrugated, with litho laminated risers. Oral-B Laboratories wanted a display with multiple retail store level applications, i.e. floorstand, side rack and end cap. The display would have common interchangeable components.

Interchangeable components allowed the display to improve inventory control, reduced freight cost and reduce tooling cost. The display has an inner tooth brush merchandiser that can hold more product in the same amount of floor space.

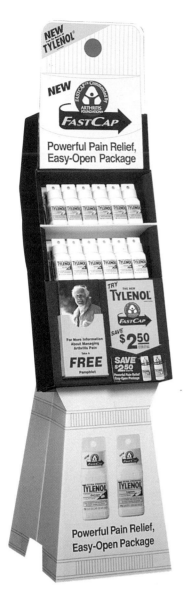

TITLE:

Tylenol "Fastcap" Launch Display

DIVISION:

Temporary

SUB-CAT:

First Aid and Pharmaceuticals

CLIENT:

McNeil Consumer Products Co.

ENTRANT:

**Chesapeake Display & Packaging Co.,
Chesapeake Corporation
Winston-Salem, NC**

AWARD:

Bronze

TITLE:

Aquafresh Flex Giant Toothbrush

DIVISION:

Permanent

SUB-CAT:

Dentifrices, Mouthwash and Oral Implements

CLIENT:

SmithKline Beecham Consumer Products

ENTRANT:

**Henschel-Steinau, Inc.
Englewood, NJ**

AWARD:

Silver

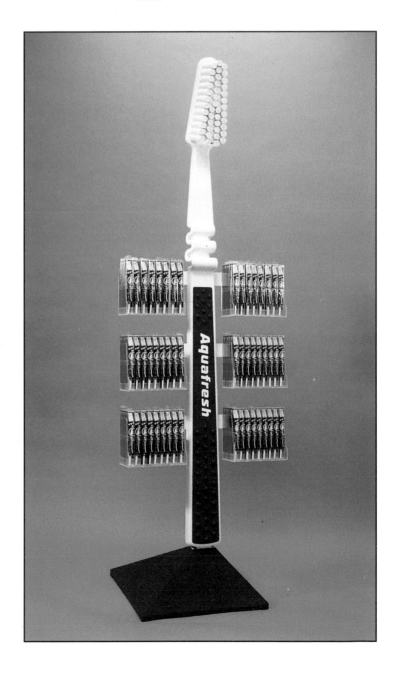

TITLE:

Oral-B Toothbrush Merchandising System

DIVISION:

Temporary

SUB-CAT:

Dentifrices, Mouthwash and Oral Implements

CLIENT:

Oral-B Laboratories

ENTRANT:

**Chesapeake Display & Packaging Co.
Chesapeake Corp.
Winston-Salem, NC**

AWARD:

Gold

TITLE:
Binaca 6 Dozen & 10 Dozen Sidekick/Floorstand

DIVISION:
Temporary

SUB-CAT:
Dentifrices, Mouthwash, and Oral Implements

CLIENT:
Reckitt & Colman, Inc.

ENTRANT:
JSC/Tri Pack,
Jefferson Smurfit Corp.
Carlstadt, NJ

AWARD:
Bronze

TITLE:

Irish Spring Deodorant Prepack Floor Stand

DIVISION:

Temporary

SUB-CAT:

Personal Hygiene, Diapers and Baby Items

CLIENT:

Mennen

ENTRANT:

Algar/The Display Connection
Clifton, NJ

AWARD:

Silver

TITLE:

Rorer-Maalox, Fibre, Floorstand/Power Wing Display

DIVISION:

Temporary

SUB-CAT:

First Aid and Pharmaceuticals

CLIENT:

Rhone-Poulenc Rorer

ENTRANT:

Packaging Corp. of America,
Trexlertown Container Plant
Lancaster, PA

AWARD:

Silver

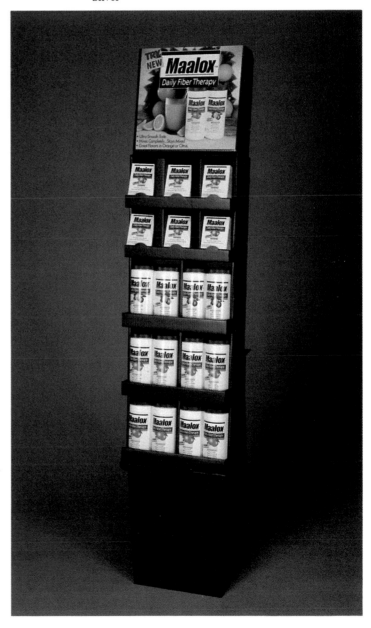

TITLE:
True Temper Garden Tool Center

DIVISION:
Permanent

SUB-CAT:
Lawn and Garden Supplies

CLIENT:
True Temper

ENTRANT:
Altwell, Inc.
Totowa, NJ

AWARD:
Gold

Altwell, Inc., Totowa, NJ, constructed a display of metal, pegboard, wire, laminated particle board and silk screening for True Temper. The display would be used in major chain stores and would hold a full line of tools weighing over 700 pounds. The display featured wheels so that it could be moved between the tool section and outdoor garden departments.

Two hundred of the displays were constructed and were to be used for a one-year period. The display cost between $100 and $250 to construct.

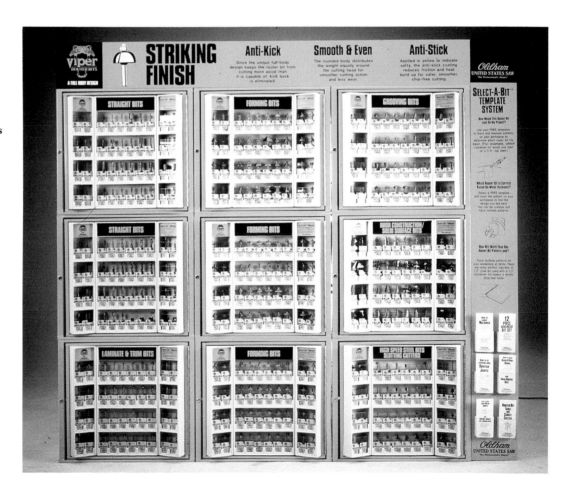

TITLE:

Pease Alert*Lock Counter Unit

DIVISION:

Permanent

SUB-CAT:

Building Supplies

CLIENT:

Pease Industries, Inc.

ENTRANT:

Diversified Advertising, Inc.
Louisville, KY

AWARD:

Silver

TITLE:

Oldham Saw Select-A-Bit
Merchandiser

DIVISION:

Permanent

SUB-CAT:

Home and Industrial Tools

CLIENT:

Oldham Saw

ENTRANT:

MCA Sign Co.
Massillon, OH

AWARD:

Silver

TITLE:

Hunter Douglas Silhouette Floor Display

DIVISION:

Permanent

SUB-CAT:

Home Furnishings and Housewares

CLIENT:

Hunter Douglas, Inc.

ENTRANT:

Thomson-Leeds Co., Inc.
New York, NY

AWARD:

Silver

TITLE:

Mannington Featured Product Display

DIVISION:

Temporary

SUB-CAT:

Home Furnishings and Housewares

CLIENT:

Mannington Resilient Floors

ENTRANT:

Art Guild, Inc.,
Display Division
West Deptford, NJ

AWARD:

Silver

TITLE:

Tarkett Decorating Idea Center (DIC)

DIVISION:

Permanent

SUB-CAT:

Home Furnishings and Housewares

CLIENT:

Tarkett, Inc.

ENTRANT:

Goldring Display Group, Inc.
Paramus, NJ

AWARD:

Gold

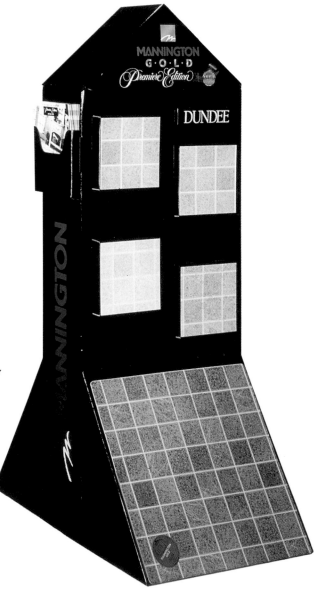

A display was needed by Tarkett, Inc., to show their full line of (320 SKUs) floor coverings. It needed to be compact, attract and hold a customer's attention, and deliver features and benefits information to the consumer on the superiority of the flooring. Goldring Display Group of Paramus, NJ, constructed a display of laminated flakeboard, styrene extrusion, fluorescent lights, backlit transparencies, silk screening and injection molding.

The display was the first in the floor covering industry to display the product by color and not by traditional product line. High impact graphics above each waterfall identified the color family. The display came complete with a color wheel so salespeople could work with the customers. Reverse sides of selling products contained product selling points and a rating of good, better or best. Sales of Tarkett product in some location have increased over 300% since the display was placed.

The display was intended to be used for a period of five to seven years. It cost over $1,000 per unit to produce. Additional production was planned because high acceptance during the first year.

TITLE:
Tarkett Commercial Idea Center (CIC)

DIVISION:
Permanent

SUB-CAT:
Home Furnishings and Housewares

CLIENT:
Tarkett, Inc.

ENTRANT:
Goldring Display Group, Inc.
Paramus, NJ

AWARD:
Bronze

TITLE:

Evercraft Air Tools Merchandising Display

DIVISION:

Permanent

SUB-CAT:

Home and Industrial Tools

CLIENT:

Napa Balkamp, Inc.

ENTRANT:

**New Dimensions Research Corp.
Melville, NY**

AWARD:

Bronze

TITLE:

Piece-A-Week Dinnerware Display

DIVISION:

Temporary

SUB-CAT:

Home Furnishings and Housewares

CLIENT:

Excel Marketing

ENTRANT:

**Al Gar/The Display Connection, Inc.
Clifton, NJ**

AWARD:

Bronze

TITLE:

Customweave Carpets Retail Environment

DIVISION:

Permanent

SUB-CAT:

Home Furnishings and Housewares

CLIENT:

Customweave Carpets

ENTRANT:

**Thomas A. Schutz Co., Inc.
Morton Grove, IL**

AWARD:

Bronze

TITLE:

**AT&T Digital 900 MHz Cordless
Telephone Introduction**

DIVISION:

Permanent

SUB-CAT:

Appliances

CLIENT:

AT&T

ENTRANT:

**Thomson-Leeds Co., Inc.
New York, NY**

AWARD:

Bronze

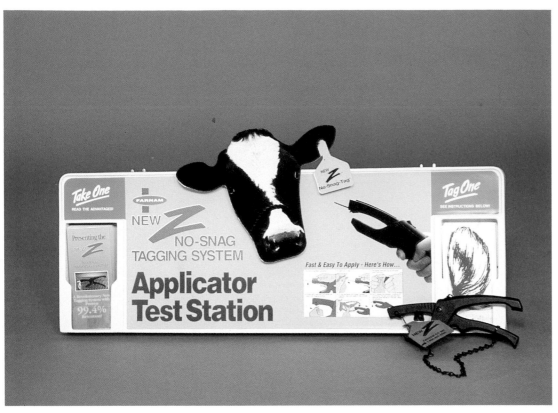

TITLE:

Farnam - No Snag Tag Test Station

DIVISION:

Permanent

SUB-CAT:

Lawn and Garden Supplies

CLIENT:

Farnam

ENTRANT:

E and E Display Group
Lawrence, KS

AWARD:

Bronze

TITLE:

Reel Lawn Mower Display Center

DIVISION:

Temporary

SUB-CAT:

Lawn and Garden Supplies

CLIENT:

American Lawn Mower Co.

ENTRANT:

Packaging Corp. of America,
Division Gas City, Indiana
Indianapolis, IN

AWARD:

Silver

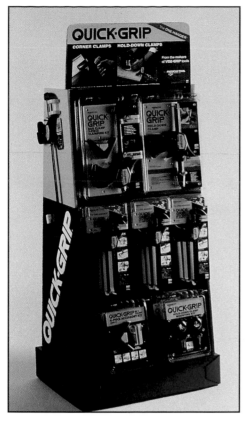

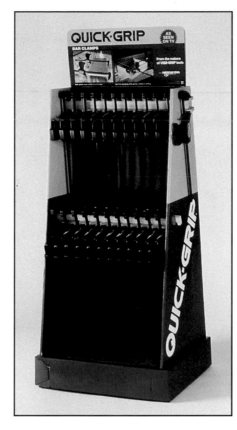

TITLE:

American Tool - Quick Grip Mini Pallet

DIVISION:

Temporary

SUB-CAT:

Home and Industrial Tools

CLIENT:

American Tool Companies, Inc.

ENTRANT:

**E and E Display Group
Lawrence, KS**

AWARD:

Gold

TITLE:

Preen/Preen N' Green Inflatable

DIVISION:

Temporary

SUB-CAT:

Lawn and Garden Supplies

CLIENT:

Greenview

ENTRANT:

**Brulene Associates, Inc.
West New York, NJ**

AWARD:

Bronze

American Tool Companies needed a display that would increase visibility of their tools to the do-it-yourselfer and be sturdy enough to be shipped overseas. The display had to encourage hands-on testing yet keep a small footprint due to limited retail floor space.

E and E Display Group, Lawrence, KS, used print tinted corrugated paperboard, flexo printed corrugated paperboard, offset printed litho mounted graphics, wood support bars, wood mini pallet, printed metal bracket and painted wood board for the display. One thousand were constructed to be used for a period of two to three months, at a cost of $25 to $50 per unit to construct.

The mini pallet allows the display to be delivered fully loaded with product for ease of set-up and positioning. Several interior structural support pieces were incorporated into the display to withstand the rigors of shipping. An open look allows the consumer to touch and use the products. Graphics on the display help educate the consumer on potential uses.

The Wells Lamont's Grip Test Center was to be placed in mass merchandisers, home centers, hardware stores and farm co-ops. The display had to be placed on existing wire racks or affixed to existing store shelves. The display had to encourage consumer trial, attract attention, illustrate the difference in products, encourage upgrade and educate the consumer on the proper size of glove.

The display fits into peg-board, slat wall and other in-store fixtures. It can be centered among an assortment of glove styles and product lines. The display captured attention by using a screwdriver-hammer handle, paint brush and a faucet handle or wing nut to encourage trying and choosing a proper size glove. The tools and the size chart encouraged the consumer in making buying decisions.

Constructed by Chesapeake Display & Packaging, Winston-Salem, NC, 500 of the units were made at a cost of $25 to $50 per display. It was design to be used for one year and constructed of vacuum formed plastic labelled with 10 point SBS. The display mounts to wire rack on a sheet metal back plate.

TITLE:
Wells Lamont "Grip Test Center" Interactive Display

DIVISION:
Permanent

SUB-CAT:
Home and Industrial Tools

CLIENT:
Wells Lamont

ENTRANT:
**Chesapeake Display & Packaging
Winston-Salem, NC**

AWARD:
Gold

TITLE:
Mannington Floor Care Center

DIVISION:
Permanent

SUB-CAT:
Home Furnishings and Housewares

CLIENT:
Mannington Resilient Floors

ENTRANT:
**Art Guild, Inc.,
Display Division
West Deptford, NJ**

AWARD:
Silver

TITLE:
Black & Decker Modular Tool System

DIVISION:
Permanent

SUB-CAT:
Home and Industrial Tools

CLIENT:
Black & Decker (U.S.), Inc.

ENTRANT:
Henschel-Steinau, Inc.
Englewood, NJ

AWARD:
Silver

TITLE:
Leviton Bulk Star Gondola Shelf Management System

DIVISION:
Permanent

SUB-CAT:
Building Supplies

CLIENT:
Leviton Mfg.

ENTRANT:
Thomson-Leeds Co. Inc.
New York, NY

AWARD:
Bronze

TITLE:
Football Borders

DIVISION:
Temporary

SUB-CAT:
Home Furnishings and Housewares

CLIENT:
F. Schumacher & Co.

ENTRANT:
**Thomson-Leeds Co., Inc.
New York, NY**

AWARD:
Bronze

TITLE:
**Big Green Clean Machine
With Mini-Video System**

DIVISION:
Permanent

SUB-CAT:
Appliances

CLIENT:
Bissell, Inc.

ENTRANT:
**RTC Industries, Inc.
Chicago, IL**

AWARD:
Silver

TITLE:

Handy Mixer Cordless Beater Display

DIVISION:

Permanent

SUB-CAT:

Appliances

CLIENT:

The Black & Decker Corp.

ENTRANT:

Trans World Marketing
East Rutherford, NJ

AWARD:

Bronze

TITLE:

Leviton Industrial Line Wall Display

DIVISION:

Permanent

SUB-CAT:

Building Supplies

CLIENT:

Leviton Mfg. Co.

ENTRANT:

Altwell, Inc.
Totowa, NJ

AWARD:

Bronze

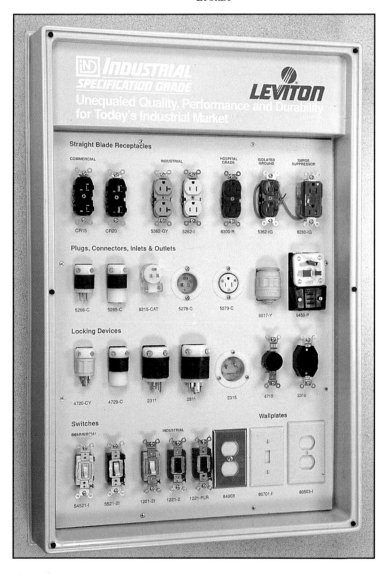

INTERNATIONAL TEMPORARY
DISPLAY OF THE YEAR

TITLE:
Atol Glasses Display

DIVISION:
Permanent

SUB-CAT:
International

CLIENT:
Atol

ENTRANT:
Prisme
Suresnes, France

AWARD:
Gold

Prisme, Suresness, France, constructed a display for Atol's glasses frame targeted towards children from four to 12 years old. Varnished and enameled wood, and steel enameled twice were used to construct 300 displays. The display was intended to be used for six months and cost between $50 and $100 to construct.

A wooden ball and colored triangle were used to evoke a funny face. A spring was used to symbolize movement, laughter and life, attracting people to play with the display. The box part of the display allowed a wide presentation of product.

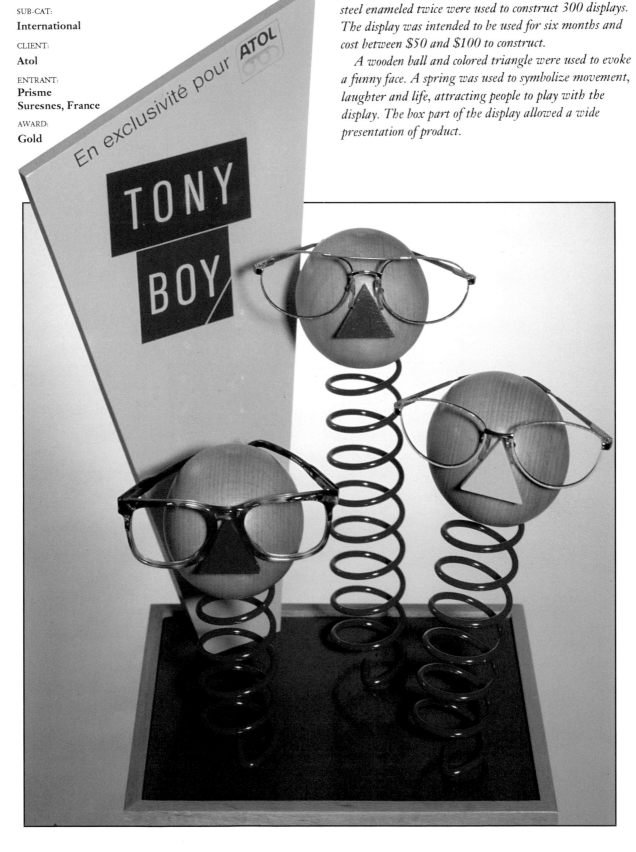

TITLE:
Kodak Floor Film Display - International

DIVISION:
Permanent

SUB-CAT:
International

CLIENT:
Kodak Brasileria Com., Ind., Ltd.

ENTRANT:
Hardsell - Brazil
New York, NY

AWARD:
Silver

TITLE:
Karacol Display - International

DIVISION:
Permanent

SUB-CAT:
International

CLIENT:
Kodak Brasileria Com. Ind. Ltd

ENTRANT:
Hardsell - Brazil
New York, NY

AWARD:
Bronze

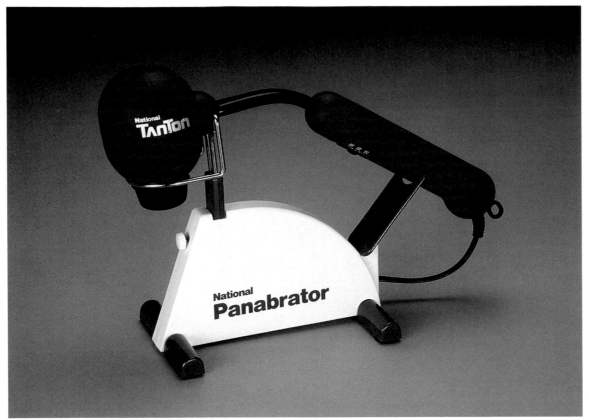

TITLE:
Panabrator Unit Display

DIVISION:
Permanent

SUB-CAT:
International

CLIENT:
Matsushita Denko Co., Ltd.

ENTRANT:
**Biko Co., Ltd.
Osaka, Japan**

AWARD:
Silver

TITLE:
Michelin's Line Of Pilot Tire Stand

DIVISION:
Permanent

SUB-CAT:
International

CLIENT:
Michelin

ENTRANT:
**Prisme
Suresnes, France**

AWARD:
Silver

TITLE:
Cartier Les Must II Prestige Display

DIVISION:
Permanent

SUB-CAT:
International

CLIENT:
Cartier

ENTRANT:
**Prisme
Suresnes, France**

AWARD:
Silver

TITLE:
Edgell Quickshot Microwave

DIVISION:
Permanent

SUB-CAT:
International

CLIENT:
Edgell Birdeye

ENTRANT:
**Visy Displays
Reservoir, Victoria, Australia**

AWARD:
Silver

TITLE:

Toilet Duck

DIVISION:

Permanent

SUB-CAT:

International

CLIENT:

S.C. Johnson & Son Pty., Ltd.

ENTRANT:

Visy Displays
Reservoir, Victoria, Australia

AWARD:

Silver

TITLE:

Max Factor "Benelux" One Metre Gondola

DIVISION:

Permanent

SUB-CAT:

International

CLIENT:

P & G Health & Beauty Care

ENTRANT:

Artform International, Inc.
Norwalk, CT

AWARD:

Silver

A display was needed by Cadbury Schweppes Pty, Ltd., to be used during non-peak selling periods. The display had to be a full gondola end display that could be set-up within 45 minutes and be reusable.

Visy Displays, Reservoir, Victoria, Australia, used corrugated board, screen printing, preprinted liner, lithographic printing, motion and sound in the display. Sales significantly increased during use of the display. Some retail outlets re-used the display up to three times for promotions.

Designed to be used for a three-week period, 800 of the displays were constructed. The display cost between $250 and $500 to construct.

TITLE:
Cadbury Carnival

DIVISION:
Permanent

SUB-CAT:
International

CLIENT:
Cadbury Schweppes Pty., Ltd.

ENTRANT:
**Visy Displays
Reservoir, Victoria,**

AWARD:
Gold

TITLE:
Provencial House Display "Le Petit Mareillais"

DIVISION:
Temporary

SUB-CAT:
International

CLIENT:
Laboratories Vendome

ENTRANT:
**Ateliers Reunis Bagnolet
Bagnolet, France**

AWARD:
Bronze

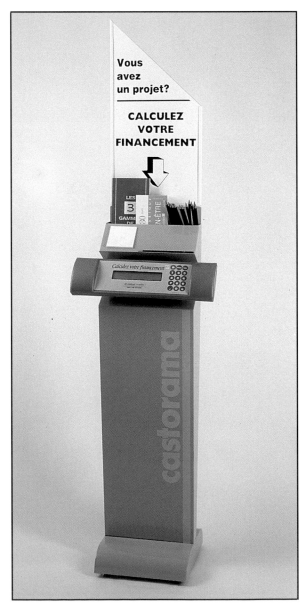

TITLE:
Cetelem Credit Simulator

DIVISION:
Permanent

SUB-CAT:
International

CLIENT:
Cetelem

ENTRANT:
**Technimage
Nimes, France**

AWARD:
Bronze

TITLE:
YokaIchi Counter P-O-P

DIVISION:
Permanent

SUB-CAT:
International

CLIENT:
Takara Shuzo Co., Ltd.

ENTRANT:
Biko Co., Ltd.
Osaka, Japan

AWARD:
Bronze

TITLE:
Moulinex - Floor Display

DIVISION:
Permanent

SUB-CAT:
International

CLIENT:
Moulinex

ENTRANT:
Futura Products GmbH
Wadern-Lockweiler, Germany

AWARD:
Bronze

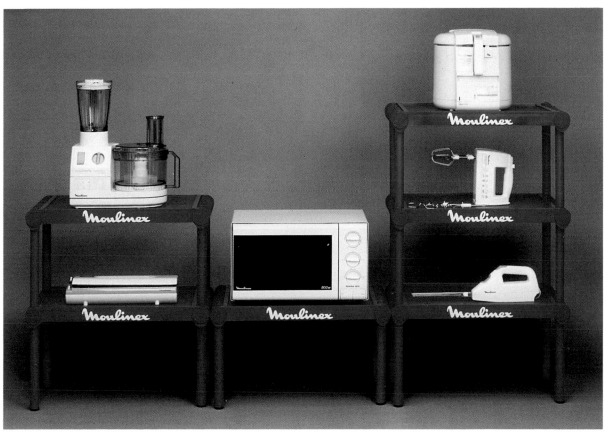

TITLE:
Dimension Shampoo Display - International

DIVISION:
Permanent

SUB-CAT:
International

CLIENT:
Unilever

ENTRANT:
Hardsell - Brazil
New York, NY

AWARD:
Silver

TITLE:
Nestle Refrigerated 'Take One' Display - International

DIVISION:
Permanent

SUB-CAT:
International

CLIENT:
Nestle Industrial E Commercial

ENTRANT:
Thomson-Leeds, Inc.
Hardsell/Brazil
New York, NY

AWARD:
Silver

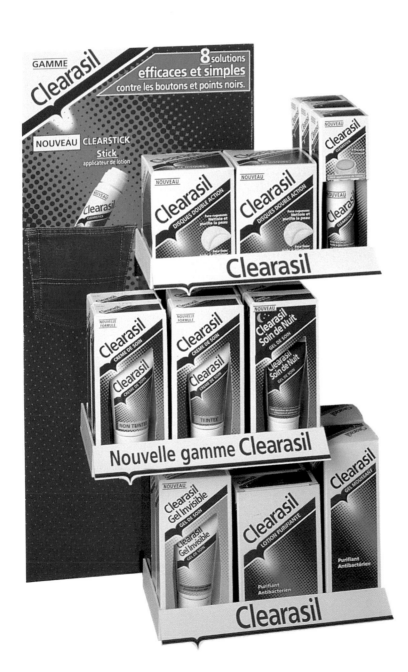

TITLE:
Clearasil Range Display

DIVISION:
Permanent

SUB-CAT:
International

CLIENT:
Procter & Gamble

ENTRANT:
**Prisme
Suresnes, France**

AWARD:
Gold

A display was needed to allow the presentation of one type of product or the entire range if needed. Procter & Gamble instructed Prisme, Suresness, France, to construct a display that would not exceed $10 per unit to construct, be used for one to three months, and a production run of 14,000 units.

Using injected polystyrene and cardboard, a modular display was created that had a tray, a super imposable spine element and a cardboard pediment. The display could be constructed in various ways depending on the amount of product. Red, white and blue were used to connect the display with the product. A minimal amount of counter space was needed for the display. The jean's pocket on the pediment targeted the product towards a younger audience.

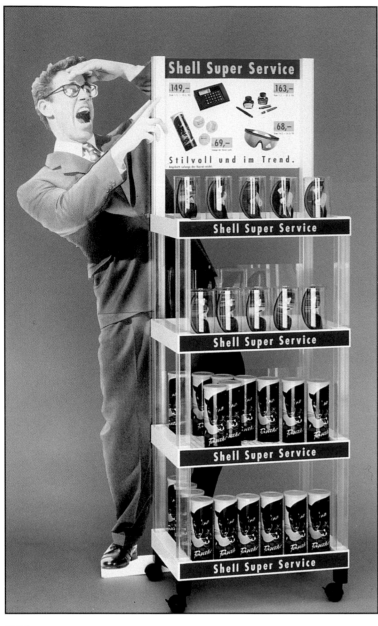

TITLE:
Shell-Shop

DIVISION:
Permanent

SUB-CAT:
International

CLIENT:
Shell Austria AG

ENTRANT:
Futura Products GmbH
Wadern-Lockweiler, Germany

AWARD:
Bronze

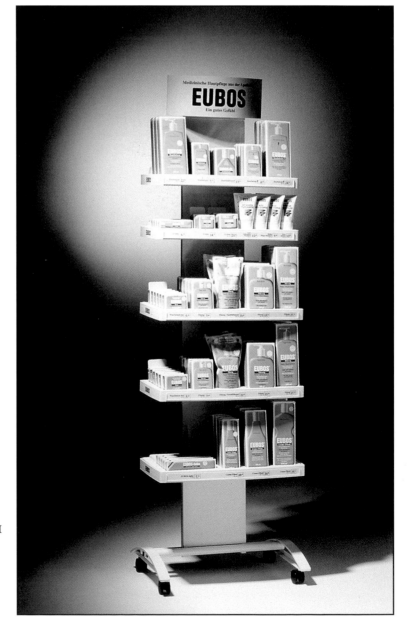

TITLE:
Eubos - Display

DIVISION:
Permanent

SUB-CAT:
International

CLIENT:
Dr. Hobein & Co. Nachf. GmbH

ENTRANT:
Plastiform Heilbronn GmbH
Heilbronn, Germany

AWARD:
Silver

INTERNATIONAL PERMANENT
DISPLAY OF THE YEAR

TITLE:
Lancome General Make Up Tester Stand

DIVISION:
Permanent

SUB-CAT:
International

CLIENT:
Lancome

ENTRANT:
Diam Decoretalage
Les Mureaux, France

AWARD:
Gold

Lancome's goal was to introduce the luxury and richness of its make-up line with the introduction of a new general tester stand. The stand also had to be a working tool to assist the cosmetician using it. Diam Decoratalage, Les Mureaux, France, constructed a display of injection mold acrylic, ABS, polycarbonate and polystyrene, fabricated plexiglass, electroplating, hot stamping, silkscreening a telescopic sliding drawer and vacuum forming. The display cost over $500 to produce with 6,000 units constructed. It was intended to be used for a period of three years.

The display utilized past successes of other displays and incorporated a larger size and more color distribution. Front and back drawers contained testers for the technician when counseling a consumer. The display was installed by company personnel and can be retrieved after use.

TITLE:
Hans Turnwald - Fine Table Accessories

DIVISION:
Permanent

SUB-CAT:
International

CLIENT:
Turnwald GmbH

ENTRANT:
Futura Products GmbH
Wardern-Lockweiler, Germany

AWARD:
Bronze

TITLE:
Benson & Hedges Tower Unit

DIVISION:
Temporary

SUB-CAT:
International

CLIENT:
W.D. & H.O. Wills (Australia)

ENTRANT:
Australian Point of Purchase Display
Warriwood, NSW, Australia

AWARD:
Bronze

TITLE:

Tria Merchandiser

DIVISION:

Permanent

SUB-CAT:

International

CLIENT:

Esselte Letraset

ENTRANT:

**Plastiform Heilbronnn GmbH
Heilbronn, Germany**

AWARD:

Silver

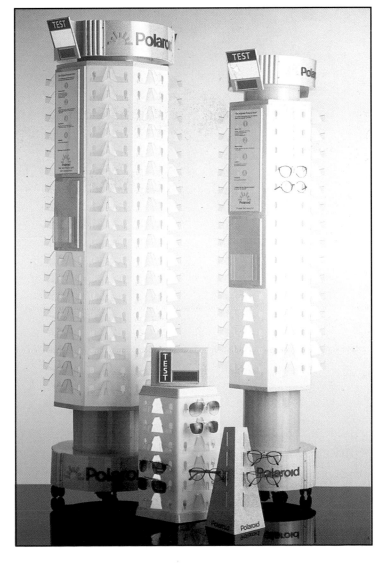

TITLE:

Polaroid Merchandiser Program

DIVISION:

Permanent

SUB-CAT:

International

CLIENT:

Polaroid Europe BV

ENTRANT:

**Tchai Displays BV
Ridderkerk, Netherlands**

AWARD:

Silver

Etti Portable Display Cart

Etti Companhia Industria E Mer required a display to re-launch a vegetable product that was previously introduced and met with limited success. Hardsell/Brazil, developed an in-store push cart that featured a changing message panel showing various pictures of the product on top. The cart contained cans of product in which a salesperson could sell along with a discount coupon. The cart was mobil and could be moved around the store to follow the crowd.

The cart was constructed of wood, a motion motor, metal and litho, and cardboard. One hundred fifty of the carts were manufactured and cost between $250 and $500 to produce. They were intended to be used for a six month period.

TITLE:
Etti Portable Display Cart - International

DIVISION:
Permanent

SUB-CAT:
International

CLIENT:
Etti Companhia Industria E Mer

ENTRANT:
Hardsell - Brazil
New York, NY

AWARD:
Gold

TITLE:
Purina Dog House Display - International

DIVISION:
Permanent

SUB-CAT:
International

CLIENT:
Purina Nutrimentos, Ltda.

ENTRANT:
Hardsell - Brazil
New York, NY

AWARD:
Bronze

TITLE:
Christian Dior Lipstick Tester

DIVISION:
Permanent

SUB-CAT:
International

CLIENT:
Christian Dior

ENTRANT:
Diam Decoretalage
Les Mureaux, France

AWARD:
Gold

Diam Decoretalage, Les Mureaux, France, was instructed by Christian Dior to construct a display for the re-introduction of the existing line of lipstick and the introduction of the new range. The display would be a forerunner for all future company displays. The shape had to allow good product presentation and be easily maintained.

The shape of the display allowed other types of product to be used in it. Injection molded plexiglass with an antistatic protective clear coating significantly reduced dust collection cleaning time. A new blue color used as the new reference of brand provided a better aspect in depth and clarity.

The display was to be used for a one-year period and 7,500 were produced. It cost between $50 and $100 per unit to construct.

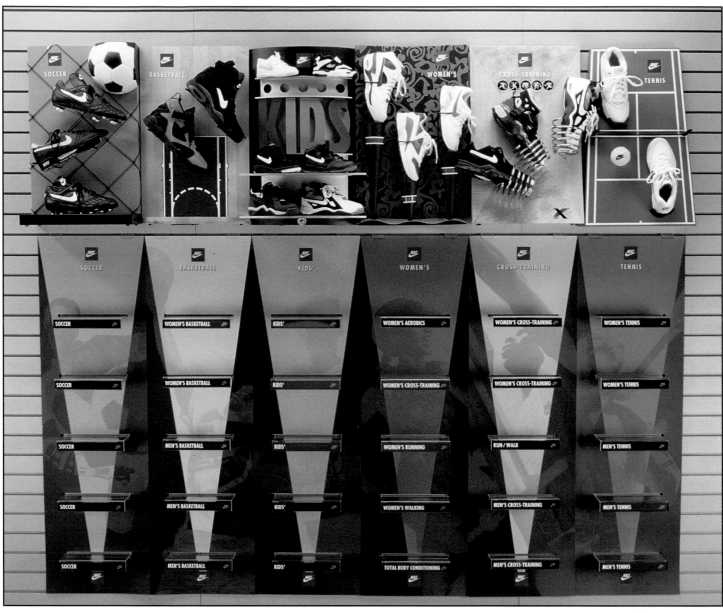

TITLE:

Nike Categorical Fixture Program

DIVISION:

Permanent

SUB-CAT:

Footware and Shoe Care

CLIENT:

Nike, Inc.

ENTRANT:

Nike, Inc.
Beaverton, OR

AWARD:

Gold

Nike, Inc., Beaverton, OR, designed a display that could be used to display an entire product collection, (i.e. basketball, running, tennis, etc.), and would allow retailers to display the collection in its own sports category, and be configured as a complete Nike collection. Therefore the display would create Nike dominance in the retail outlet.

The company created a display that was a system of different displays for each category, but could be put together to create a strong fixture with visual impact. Each category could be used individually if the retailer wished. Keeping with tradition, symbols of individual sports were used with each category of shoe.

Nike used vacuum forming, injection molding, urethane molding, wood, metal, fabric, silk screening and lithography in constructing the display. It was intended to be used for 18 months and 1,500 units were constructed. The display system cost between $100 and $250 to build.

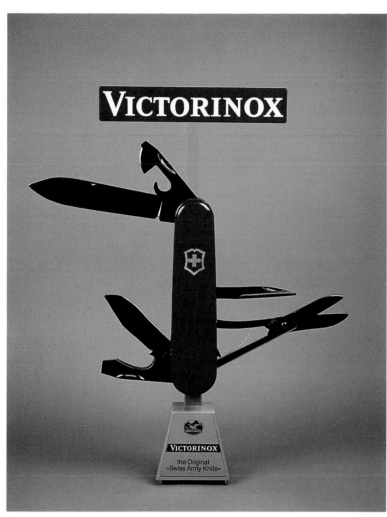

TITLE:
Victorinox Swiss Army Motion Display

DIVISION:
Permanent

SUB-CAT:
Jewelry

CLIENT:
Victorinox

ENTRANT:
**Thomson-Leeds Company, Inc.
New York, NY**

AWARD:
Silver

TITLE:
**Michael Jordan/Bugs Bunny/Marvin The
Martian Stand-Up Cut-Out**

DIVISION:
Permanent

SUB-CAT:
Footware and Shoe Care

CLIENT:
Nike, Inc.

ENTRANT:
**Rapid Mounting and Finishing Co.,
California Division
Union City, CA**

AWARD:
Bronze

TITLE:
Coats & Clark Counter & Hanging Merchandiser

DIVISION:
Permanent

SUB-CAT:
Apparel and Sewing Notions

CLIENT:
Coats & Clark

ENTRANT:
Dauman Displays
New York, NY

AWARD:
Silver

TITLE:
Ray Ban Collection

DIVISION:
Permanent

SUB-CAT:
Jewelry

CLIENT:
Bausch & Lomb, Inc.

ENTRANT:
Dauman Displays, Inc.
New YorK, NY

AWARD:
Silver

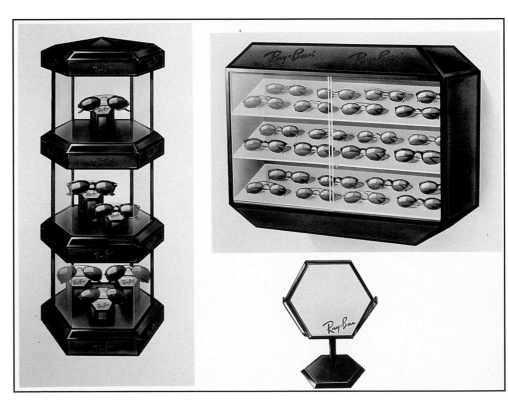

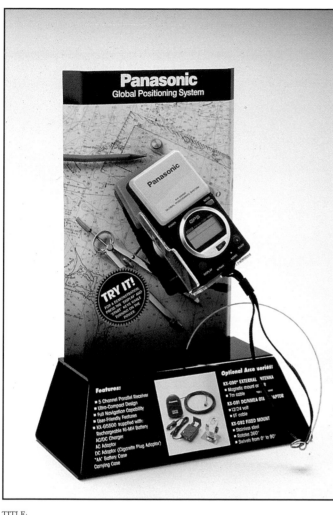

TITLE:

Panasonic Global Positioning System Counter Unit

DIVISION:

Permanent

SUB-CAT:

Fine Items and Cameras

CLIENT:

Panasonic

ENTRANT:

**Al Gar/The Display Connection, Inc.
Clifton, NJ**

AWARD:

Bronze

TITLE:

Nike Air Max Program

DIVISION:

Permanent

SUB-CAT:

Footware and Shoe Care

CLIENT:

Nike, Inc.

ENTRANT:

**DCI Marketing
Milwaukee, WI**

AWARD:

Bronze

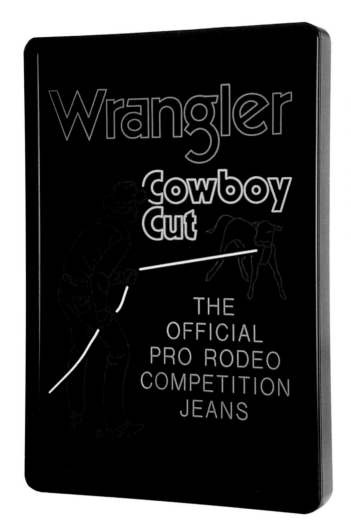

TITLE:
Wrangler Cowboy Cut Backlit Display

DIVISION:
Permanent

SUB-CAT:
Apparel and Sewing Notions

CLIENT:
Wrangler

ENTRANT:
Clearr Corp.
Minnetonka, MN

AWARD:
Silver

TITLE:
Nautica Wall and Counter Signs/ Nautica International

DIVISION:
Permanent

SUB-CAT:
Apparel and Sewing Notions

CLIENT:
Nautica Apparel International

ENTRANT:
Big Apple Sign Corp.
New York, NY

AWARD:
Bronze

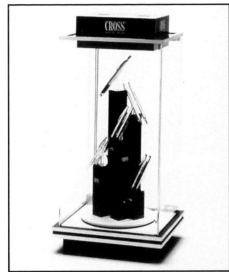

TITLE:
A.T. Cross Global Merchandising Display System

DIVISION:
Permanent

SUB-CAT:
Jewelry

CLIENT:
A.T. Cross Co.

ENTRANT:
**Thomas A. Schutz Co., Inc.,
Eastern Division
Westport, CT**

AWARD:
Gold

A display to be used in department stores, gift stores, pen stores, stationery stores and jewelry stores was required by A.T. Cross Company. The display had to increase market penetration domestically and internationally, reinforce the high quality image, and present a consistent universal identity for the Cross brand.

The display consisted of 25 elements and allowed individual retailers to create custom displays. Elements could be interchanged depending on individual retailer requirements. Green and gold coloring was used to reinforce the image of high quality. Quinel fabric was used for its ease of care and washability, and gold fleck was mixed with green styrene to increase the perception of quality.

Thomas A. Schutz Co., Westport, CT, used injection molded high impact styrene, vacuum forming, metal fabrication, lithography, hot stamping and low voltage illumination when constructing 2,500 of the displays. The display had a cost of over $500 per display to build and an intended use of two years.

153

TITLE:

Spring 1993 Sandal Pak P.O.P.

DIVISION:

Permanent

SUB-CAT:

Footware and Shoes Care

CLIENT:

Nike, Inc.

ENTRANT:

**Rapid Mounting and Finishing Co.,
California Division
Union City, CA**

AWARD:

Silver

TITLE:

Elegance 4 Way Column

DIVISION:

Permanent

SUB-CAT:

Apparel and Sewing Notions

CLIENT:

Exquisite Form Industries

ENTRANT:

**Melrose Displays, Inc.
Passaic, NJ**

AWARD:

Bronze

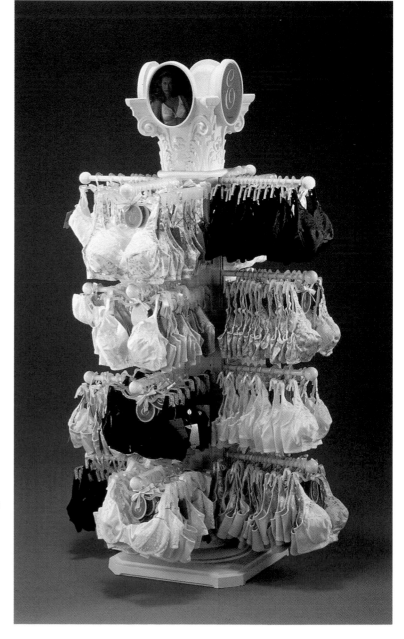

TITLE:
Nike Air Huarache Plus

DIVISION:
Permanent

SUB-CAT:
Footware and Shoe Care

CLIENT:
Nike, Inc.

ENTRANT:
**Frank Mayer & Associates, Inc.
Grafton, WI**

AWARD:
Bronze

TITLE:
Burlington Rotary

DIVISION:
Permanent

SUB-CAT:
Apparel and Sewing Notions

CLIENT:
Kayser-Roth Hosiery

ENTRANT:
**New Dimensions Research Corp.
Melville, NY**

AWARD:
Bronze

TITLE:
Disney Tee Stand

DIVISION:
Permanent

SUB-CAT:
Apparel and Sewing Notions

CLIENT:
Mamiye Bros.

ENTRANT:
**Miller/Zell, Inc.
Atlanta, GA**

AWARD:
Silver

TITLE:
Nike Holiday '92 Flight P-O-P

DIVISION:
Permanent

SUB-CAT:
Footware and Shoe Care

CLIENT:
Nike, Inc.

ENTRANT:
**DCI Marketing
Milwaukee, WI**

AWARD:
Bronze

TITLE:

Hiking Boot "Mountain" Display

DIVISION:

Permanent

SUB-CAT:

Footware and Shoe Care

CLIENT:

Fila U.S.A.

ENTRANT:

R.E.A. Display
Fairfield, NJ

AWARD:

Gold

R.E.A. Display, Fairfield, NJ, constructed a display for Fila, U.S.A. that would hold nine boots and could be approached from all sides. The display had to portray the company's product as a leader in the outdoor/hiking boot market. The display would be placed in athletic specialty stores and shoe stores.

The display was constructed of a acrythane spray-in-place/insta-set urethane casting system and 722 rub-in-place stain coloring system. The display was intended to be used for two years and cost between $100 and $250 to construct.

TITLE:

New Balance Modular Panel System

DIVISION:

Permanent

SUB-CAT:

Footware and Shoe Care

CLIENT:

New Balance Athletic Shoe Co.

ENTRANT:

Thomson-Leeds Co., Inc.
New York, NY

AWARD:

Bronze

TITLE:
Reebok "Kids" General Merchandising Display

DIVISION:
Permanent

SUB-CAT:
Footware and Shoe Care

CLIENT:
Reebok International

ENTRANT:
**RTC East,
A Division of RTC Industries
New York, NY**

AWARD:
Bronze

TITLE:
Sears "Walking" Shoe Display

DIVISION:
Permanent

SUB-CAT:
Footware and Shoe Care

CLIENT:
Reebok International

ENTRANT:
**RTC East,
A Division of RTC Industries
New York, NY**

AWARD:
Bronze

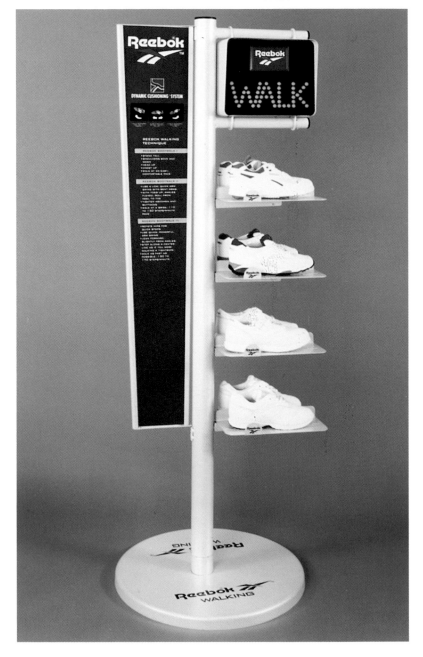

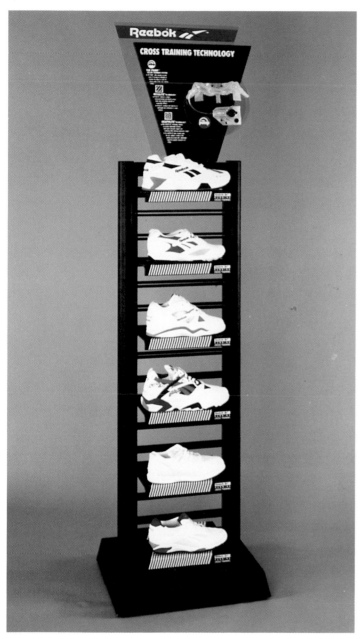

TITLE:

Reebok Foot Action "Back to School" Merchandising Kit

DIVISION:

Temporary

SUB-CAT:

Footware and Shoe Care

CLIENT:

Reebok International

ENTRANT:

**RTC East,
A Division of RTC Industries
New York, NY**

AWARD:

Silver

TITLE:

Lady Foot Locker/Reebok Planet Reebok

DIVISION:

Temporary

SUB-CAT:

Footware and Shoe Care

CLIENT:

Lady Foot Locker

ENTRANT:

**Medallion Associates, Ltd.
New York, NY**

AWARD:

Bronze

TITLE:
Foot Locker/Nike - "Air"

DIVISION:
Temporary

SUB-CAT:
Footware and Shoe Care

CLIENT:
Foot Locker

ENTRANT:
**Medallion Associates, Ltd.
New York, NY**

AWARD:
Silver

TITLE:
Foot Locker/Nike - "Flight"

DIVISION:
Temporary

SUB-CAT:
Footware and Shoe Care

CLIENT:
Foot Locker

ENTRANT:
**Medallion Associates, Ltd.
New York, NY**

AWARD:
Bronze

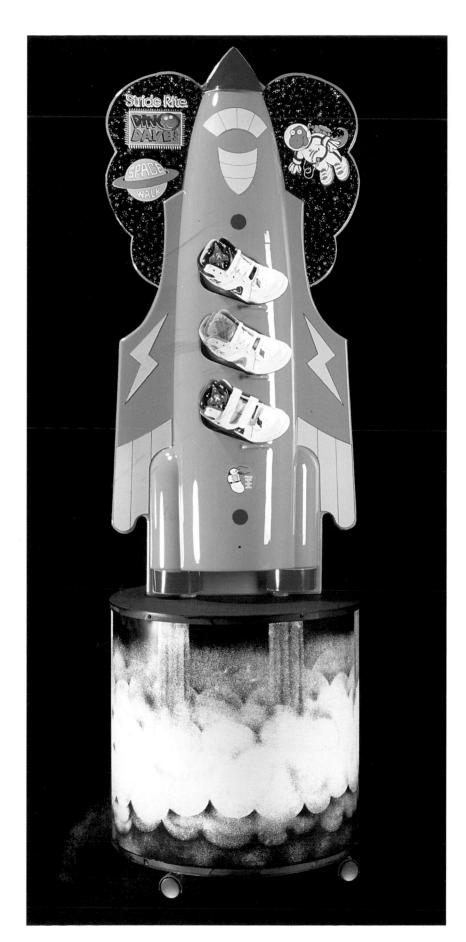

TITLE:
Stride Rite Space Walk Rocket Ship

DIVISION:
Temporary

SUB-CAT:
Footware and Shoe Care

CLIENT:
Stride Rite

ENTRANT:
Display Masters
Long Island City, NY

AWARD:
Gold

A new kid's sneaker was introduced by Stride Rite that had a voice chip in the tongue of the shoe that made a rocket ship sound, and an LED that flashed. A display was needed that reinforced the new shoe, be used at the front of mall shoe stores, and not use an electrical cord because of tripping hazard.

Display Masters, Long Island City, NY, created a display resembling the rocket ship that attracted attention of kids and parents. It utilized a motion detector to set off 15 seconds of LED lights in the nose and rocket ship sounds. A four D-cell battery pack provided 50,000 cycles. Product is screwed into place permanently from the inside to deter theft. Fiber tubes were used to connect the base to the rocket, that were shipped separately.

Vacuum forming, silk screening, labels and corrugated back, fiber tubes, injection molded base caps and wheels, silk screened styrene base wrap, motion sensors with sound, chipboard base and a battery pack were used in the construction. One thousand of the displays were created to be used for a three-month time period. It cost between $100 and $250 to construct.

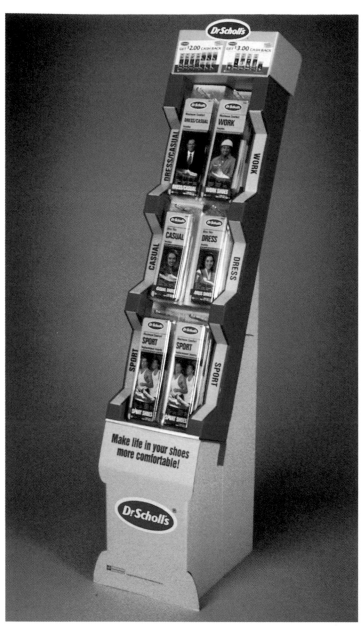

TITLE:
Dr. Scholl's Premium Insole Floor Stand/Power Wing 36 pc.

DIVISION:
Temporary

SUB-CAT:
Footware and Shoe Care

CLIENT:
Schering-Plough

ENTRANT:
**Packaging Corporation of America,
Trexlertown Container Plant
Trexlertown, PA**

AWARD:
Silver

TITLE:
Reebok Graphlite Slatwall

DIVISION:
Temporary

SUB-CAT:
Footware and Shoe Care

CLIENT:
Reebok International, Ltd.

ENTRANT:
**Thomson-Leeds Co., Inc.
New York, NY**

AWARD:
Bronze

TITLE:

Reebok Shaq Tower

DIVISION:

Temporary

SUB-CAT:

Footware and Shoe Care

CLIENT:

Reebok International

ENTRANT:

**Thomson-Leeds Co., Inc.
New York, NY**

AWARD:

Silver

TITLE:

Reebok Hardcourt Floor

DIVISION:

Temporary

SUB-CAT:

Footware and Shoe Care

CLIENT:

Reebok International, Ltd.

ENTRANT:

**Thomson-Leeds Co., Inc.
New York, NY**

AWARD:

Gold

*A display to be used in athletic footwear stores was
needed to introduce a new line of tennis sneakers to an
upscale market. Reebok International had Thomson-
Leeds Co., Inc., New York, NY, construct the display.*

*Using metal mesh, silkscreening EPS foam, polyure-
thane and foam hardware, 750 displays were created. A
mini tennis court was created with a metal frame and
nylon netting with a tennis ball being used as the base.
The display communicated to the consumer that the
product was a rugged tennis shoe and had Reebok
quality. The display had a small footprint that was well
received by retailers.*

*Intended to be used for six months, the display cost
between $50 and $100 to produce.*

TEMPORARY DISPLAY OF THE YEAR

TITLE:

L.A. Lights Skateboard Shoe Shelf

DIVISION:

Permanent

SUB-CAT:

Footware and Shoe Care

CLIENT:

L.A. Gear

ENTRANT:

The Elliott Group
Pawtucket, RI

AWARD:

Bronze

TITLE:

Fruit Of The Loom Back To School Display

DIVISION:

Temporary

SUB-CAT:

Apparel and Sewing Notions

CLIENT:

Fruit Of The Loom

ENTRANT:

Leggett & Platt
Masterack
Atlanta, GA

AWARD:

Bronze

TITLE:
Champs Sports/Nike "Back to School"

DIVISION:
Temporary

SUB-CAT:
Footware and Shoe Care

CLIENT:
Champs Sports

ENTRANT:
**Medallion Associates, Ltd
New York, NY**

AWARD:
Bronze

TITLE:
Hanes Back-to-School Pallet Promo

DIVISION:
Temporary

SUB-CAT:
Apparel and Sewing Notions

CLIENT:
Sara Lee Knit Products

ENTRANT:
**Decision Point Marketing
Winston-Salem, NC**

AWARD:
Bronze

SALES PROMOTION OF THE YEAR

TITLE:	TITLE:
Bud Bowl V	**Bud Family St. Partick's Day**
DIVISION:	DIVISION:
National	**National**
SUB-CAT:	SUB-CAT:
National	**National**
CLIENT:	CLIENT:
Anheuser-Busch, Inc.	**Anheuser-Busch, Inc.**
ENTRANT:	ENTRANT:
Anheuser-Busch, Inc.	**Anheuser-Busch, Inc.**
St. Louis, MO	**St. Louis, MO**
AWARD:	AWARD:
Gold	**Bronze**

Anheuser-Busch, Inc., St. Louis, MO, used the Bud Bowl promotion to carry over strong beer sales from December through January, and to capitalize on the Super Bowl. A high value prize also would be accompanying the promotion and be advertised via point-of-sale, magazines, radio and television.

Total budget for the promotion was over $1 million and would take place over a four-week period. The cost to construct the P-O-P display was between $25 and $50 per unit. Litho printed and die cut mounted stock, vacuum forming, an electric motor and printed vinyl were used in the construction of the program.

The in-store promotion featured a simulated football field, banners, danglers, case card and a stand-up bottle with a football helmet. A $1 million dollar sweepstakes was to be given away during the game and was promoted within the display.

TITLE:
**Mobile Display Unit (MDU)
For Bar Soaps**

DIVISION:
National

SUB-CAT:
National

CLIENT:
Procter and Gamble Co.

ENTRANT:
**The Dyment Co.
Cincinnati, OH**

AWARD:
Gold

TITLE:
Food Barn Bingo

DIVISION:
Regional

SUB-CAT:
Regional

CLIENT:
Food Barn

ENTRANT:
**Frank Mayer & Associates, Inc.
Grafton, WI**

AWARD:
Bronze

*Procter and Gamble Company's promotion was to be
used in grocery, mass merchandising and drug stores.
The promotion was deployed on all P&G bar soap
brands and sizes to meet various needs of the consumer.
The promotion was an alternative to the usual dump
bin that was used in the past for soap displays.*

*The Dyment Company, Cincinnati, OH, constructed
the display of corrugated board, flexo printed and die
cut, four-color process lithography mounted and die cut.
Wheel and axle assemblies were assembled of high
impact molded styrene. It cost between $10 and $15 to
construct with 10,000 units produced. The total
promotion budget was under $500,000 and lasted for
six weeks. Other promotion techniques used included
promotional special packs and sampling.*

TITLE:

Motorola Digital Live Product Display

DIVISION:

Permanent

SUB-CAT:

Professional

CLIENT:

Motorola

ENTRANT:

**Benchmarc Display, Inc.
Vernon Hills, IL**

AWARD:

Bronze

TITLE:

Motorola Multi Pager Modular Merchandiser

DIVISION:

Permanent

SUB-CAT:

Professional

CLIENT:

Motorola, Inc.

ENTRANT:

**Visual Marketing, Inc.
Chicago, IL**

AWARD:

Silver

TITLE:

"Live Newscenter"

DIVISION:

Permanent

SUB-CAT:

Other Services and Establishments

ENTRANT:

**AG Industries/Visual Dynamics,
American Greetings Corp.
Cleveland, OH**

AWARD:

Gold

AG Industries/Visual Dynamics, American Greetings Corp., Cleveland, OH, developed a display to be used in outlets that generated between $20,000 and $50,000 per week. The display had to provide an organized way to merchandise multiple title news publications under one end cap, and to have the top three to four headlines on a daily basis displayed through an L.E.D. display.

Advertising spots were sold due to the fact that the display could illuminate color transparencies with a 30 second message on the L.E.D. Top headlines were received via a wireless receiver and transmitted via satellite. The display was designed as a 47"x24" end-cap to fit within most supermarket restrictions. Merchandising bins incorporated a 15 degree forward angle, as well as a 4" wide front slot that allowed excellent presentation of product.

The unit was designed to be used for a three- to five-year period at a cost of over $1,000 per unit. It was constructed of pattern perforated sheet metal blanks break press formed to shape, powder-coat painted and silk screened I.D. particle board with high pressure laminate color, CNC router cut to size, and rotationally molded polypropylene bins. A total of 250 units were produced.

TITLE:
Under The Counter SURPRISE-SURPRISE Display

DIVISION:
Permanent

SUB-CAT:
Quick Service Food Restaurants

CLIENT:
Little Caesars Enterprises, Inc.

ENTRANT:
**KCS Industries, Inc.,
Banta Corp.
Milwaukee, WI**

AWARD:
Bronze

TITLE:
Beauty and the Beast

DIVISION:
Temporary

SUB-CAT:
Quick Service Food Restaurants

CLIENT:
Pizza Hut, Inc.

ENTRANT:
**Phoenix Display and Packaging Corp.,
National Packaging Corp.
West Deptford, NJ**

AWARD:
Silver

TITLE:

K-Mart Islander Cafe Menu Sign

DIVISION:

Permanent

SUB-CAT:

Quick Service Food Restaurants

CLIENT:

K-Mart Corp.

ENTRANT:

**Ridan Displays, Inc.
Ronkonkoma, NY**

AWARD:

Silver

TITLE:

Hot 'n Now Drive-Thru Order Station

DIVISION:

Permanent

SUB-CAT:

Quick Service Food Restaurants

CLIENT:

Hot n' Now, Inc.

ENTRANT:

**Everbrite, Inc.,
Subsidiary-GHN
Greenfield, WI**

AWARD:

Silver

TITLE:
United Parcel Service - Next Generation Indoor Letter Center

DIVISION:
Permanent

SUB-CAT:
Professional

CLIENT:
U.P.S. - Indoor Letter Center

ENTRANT:
**AG Industries,
American Greetings Corp.
Cleveland, OH**

AWARD:
Silver

TITLE:
Leaps and Bounds Identification Program

DIVISION:
Permanent

SUB-CAT:
Other Services and Establishments

CLIENT:
Leaps and Bounds, Inc.

ENTRANT:
**Everbrite, Inc.,
Division - ISD
Greenfield, WI**

AWARD:
Bronze

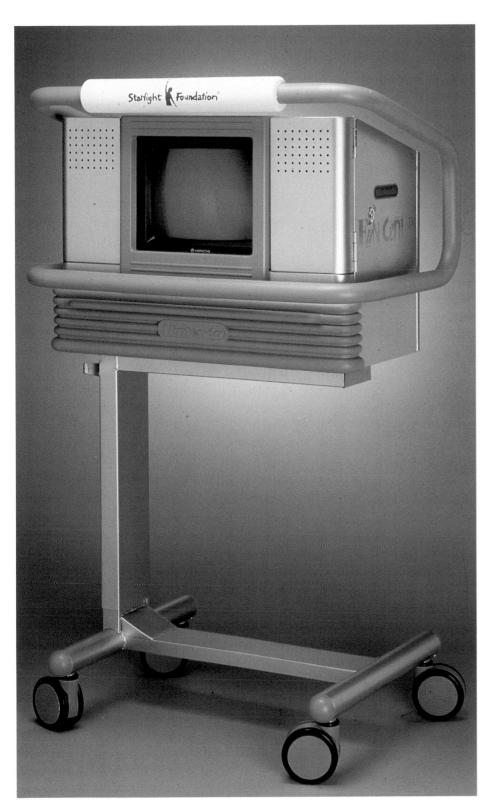

TITLE:
The Starlight Foundation/Nintendo Portable Fun Center

DIVISION:
Permanent

SUB-CAT:
Other Services and Establishments

CLIENT:
The Starlight Foundation

ENTRANT:
Nintendo Of America Inc.
Redmond, WA

AWARD:
Gold

The Starlight Foundation in conjunction with Nintendo of America, Inc., Redmond, WA, created a display that would be used on the captive audience in hospitals, and divert from the pain and tedium usually associated with a hospital stay. The video unit was able to play the most popular video games, as well as video movies. The goal was to show off the latest games, and after the patient left the hospital he/she would go and purchase the games. The unit had to be able to go right to a hospital bed requiring mobility and proper height.

Six hundred of the fun centers were constructed with a tremendous success among not only patients, but professional staff as well. The display is attributed with the use of less pain medications when patients are occupied with the video system. Constructed of steel housings, gas-assisted shocks, vacuum-formed componentry, custom stereo sounds and electronic packaging, the unit cost over $1,000 per display to build. Each unit is expected to be used for a period of two years.

TITLE:

Busch Gardens Logo Neon

DIVISION:

Permanent

SUB-CAT:

Professional

CLIENT:

Anheuser-Busch, Inc.

ENTRANT:

**Everbrite, Inc.,
Subsidiary-GHN
Greenfield, WI**

AWARD:

Bronze

TITLE:

American Express - Moneygram (Large)

DIVISION:

Permanent

SUB-CAT:

Professional

CLIENT:

First Data Corp.

ENTRANT:

**Everbrite, Inc.,
Subsidiary - GHN
Greenfield, WI**

AWARD:

Bronze

TITLE:

Newton Demo Display

DIVISION:

Temporary

SUB-CAT:

Professional

CLIENT:

CKS Partners/Apple Computer, Inc.

ENTRANT:

Robert Nielsen & Associates, Ltd.
Rolling Meadows, IL

AWARD:

Bronze

TITLE:

California Lottery Merchandising Program

DIVISION:

Permanent

SUB-CAT:

Other Services and Establishments

CLIENT:

California Lottery

ENTRANT:

California Lottery
Sacramento, CA

AWARD:

Bronze

TITLE:
Nabisco - Christmas Display

DIVISION:
Temporary

SUB-CAT:
Snacks, Cookies and Crackers

CLIENT:
Nabisco Biscuit Co.

ENTRANT:
**Displays Unlimited, Inc.
Richmond, VA**

AWARD:
Bronze

TITLE:
Pepsi Cube Motion Display

DIVISION:
Temporary

SUB-CAT:
Soft Drinks, Mineral Waters, and Powdered Mixes

CLIENT:
Pepsi-Cola Co.

ENTRANT:
**Great Northern Corp.,
Display Group
Racine, WI**

AWARD:
Silver

TITLE:
Care Free Counter Display

DIVISION:
Permanent

SUB-CAT:
Candy, Gum and Mints

CLIENT:
Planters Lifesavers Co.

ENTRANT:
**Decision Point Marketing
Winston-Salem, NC**

AWARD:
Gold

A display was needed to implement Planter Lifesavers Company's new Care Free line of gum. The display had to be easily implemented by the sales force in the field, display all flavors, require limited space, provide for permanent graphics and was lightweight.

A display utilizing powder-coated wire and screen printed hardboard core plastic extrusions was manufactured. It was constructed by Decision Point Marketing, Winston-Salem, NC. The display required no tools to install, weighed only 12 pounds, and required only ten minutes to install. The display used only one square-foot of space and shelf angles ensured product boxes remained fronted and product would feed forward.

The display was intended to be used for a six-month period and cost between $50 and $100 to construct. One thousand displays were built.

TITLE:

Brach's Next Generation 24 Bin End Cap

DIVISION:

Permanent

SUB-CAT:

Candy, Gum and Mints

CLIENT:

E.J. Brach Corp.

ENTRANT:

AMD Industries Inc.
Chicago, IL

AWARD:

Bronze

TITLE:

Hostess Futura Cadillac Gondola

DIVISION:

Permanent

SUB-CAT:

Snacks, Cookies, and Crackers

CLIENT:

Contintental Baking Co.

ENTRANT:

Chicago Display Co.
Melrose Park, IL

AWARD:

Silver

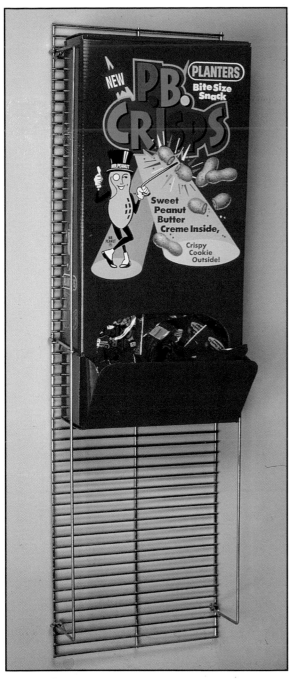

TITLE:

P.B. Crisps Trial Size Power Wing Dump

DIVISION:

Temporary

SUB-CAT:

Snacks, Cookies and Crackers

CLIENT:

Planters LifeSavers Co.

ENTRANT:

Al Gar/The Display Connection, Inc.
Clifton, NJ

AWARD:

Bronze

TITLE:

Brach's Snack Collection Counter Display

DIVISION:

Permanent

SUB-CAT:

Candy, Gum and Mints

CLIENT:

E.J. Brach Corp.

ENTRANT:

Chicago Show
Morton Grove, IL

AWARD:

Bronze

TITLE:
Frito-Lay "Chip City" Display

DIVISION:
Permanent

SUB-CAT:
Snacks, Cookies and Crackers

CLIENT:
Frito-Lay

ENTRANT:
Mechtronics Corp.
Stamford, CT

AWARD:
Gold

Mechtronics Corp., Stamford, CT, constructed a display for Frito-Lay that marketed all popular products offered by the client. The Chester Cheetah character was used as the spokesperson to attract kids. The display allowed consumers to select their own multi-pack and also merchandised the popular 25-cent sizes.

The display was constructed by using tubular steel frame, fabricated styrene and vacuum formed distortion printed styrene. It cost over $500 per unit to construct and was intended to be used for a two-year period. Five hundred of the Chip City merchandisers were built.

TITLE:
Coca-Cola Fastlane II

DIVISION:
Permanent

SUB-CAT:
Soft Drinks, Mineral Waters and Powdered Mixes

CLIENT:
Coca-Cola USA

ENTRANT:
**Mead Merchandising,
The Mead Corp.
Atlanta, GA**

AWARD:
Silver

TITLE:
Frito-Lay Bread Table

DIVISION:
Permanent

SUB-CAT:
Snacks, Cookies and Crackers

CLIENT:
Pepsico, Inc.

ENTRANT:
**DCI Marketing
Milwaukee, WI**

AWARD:
Silver

TITLE:
Frito-Lay Expressmate w/Salsa Shelf

DIVISION:
Permanent

SUB-CAT:
Snacks, Cookies and Crackers

CLIENT:
Pepsico, Inc.

ENTRANT:
**DCI Marketing
Milwaukee, WI**

AWARD:
Bronze

TITLE:
Hershey's Hugs/Multi-Use Display

DIVISION:
Temporary

SUB-CAT:
Candy, Gum and Mints

CLIENT:
Hershey Chocolate USA

ENTRANT:
**Markson Rosenthal & Co.
Englewood Cliffs, NJ**

AWARD:
Silver

TITLE:
The 1993 "New Stage" Merchandising Program

DIVISION:
Permanent

SUB-CAT:
Soft Drinks, Mineral Waters and Powdered Mixes

CLIENT:
Coca-Cola USA

ENTRANT:
Coca-Cola USA
Atlanta, GA

AWARD:
Bronze

TITLE:

Ripplins Display

DIVISION:

Temporary

SUB-CAT:

Snacks, Cookies and Crackers

CLIENT:

Keebler Co.

ENTRANT:

**Packaging Corp. of America
Burlington, WI**

AWARD:

Bronze

TITLE:

Mistle Toad Candy Display

DIVISION:

Temporary

SUB-CAT:

Candy, Gum, and Mints

CLIENT:

Edward Sarson Productions

ENTRANT:

**Packaging Corp. of America,
Division Gas City, Indiana
Indianapolis, IN**

AWARD:

Bronze

TITLE:
Elephant/Tiger Barnum Tower Display

DIVISION:
Temporary

SUB-CAT:
Snacks, Cookies and Crackers

CLIENT:
Nabisco Brands, Inc.

ENTRANT:
Conocraft, Inc.
Sussex, NJ

AWARD:
Gold

Conocraft, Inc., Sussex, NJ, created a display for Nabisco Brands to heighten awareness of Barnum's Animal Crackers among kids. The display had to generate higher profits, appear full at all times, and bring a newness to the Barnum animal merchandising efforts.

The display was very well received by retailers that lead to a longer use for the display than the originally anticipated four weeks. The display also was attributed with stronger sales of the product over the previous year. Ten thousand of the displays were constructed.

Conocraft used die-cut corrugated board with acrylic and ultra-violet coatings. The display had a construction cost of $10 to $15 per unit.

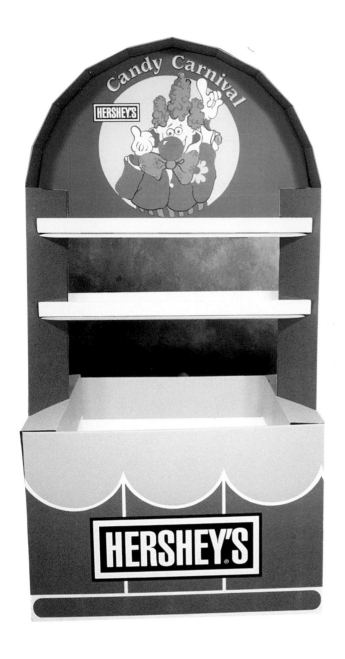

TITLE:
Candy Carnival Display

DIVISION:
Temporary

SUB-CAT:
Candy, Gum and Mints

CLIENT:
Hershey Chocolate USA

ENTRANT:
**Chesapeake Display,
Chesapeake Corp.
Winston-Salem, NC**

AWARD:
Bronze

TITLE:
Perugina Stacking Spring-Load Racks

DIVISION:
Permanent

SUB-CAT:
Candy, Gum and Mints

CLIENT:
Perugina Chocolate & Confections

ENTRANT:
**Greater Display, Inc.
Warwick, NJ**

AWARD:
Silver

TITLE:
Kid's Pack Display

DIVISION:
Temporary

SUB-CAT:
Snacks, Cookies and Crackers

CLIENT:
Pepperidge Farm, Inc.

ENTRANT:
Stone Container Corp.
Richmond, VA

AWARD:
Gold

Pepperidge Farm wanted a display that would capital-
ize on the children under 12-years-old market for their
Gold Fish product. The display also had to create
incentive to sample product, hold two cases of product,
provide recognition of the corporate name and be easy to
set up.

Stone Container Corp., Richmond, VA, created a
display of 200 pound BWIS corrugated paper with
flexographic printing. Using colorful graphics in the
shape of a large goldfish, and a net-like bin to contain
the product, the display succeeded in the company's
goals. The net used gravity feed to keep the display full
and a low height made it accessible to children. The
display consisted of three-pieces and was easy to set-up.

The company constructed 13,000 of the displays at a
cost of $10 to $15 per unit. It was intended to be used
for a number of months.

TITLE:

Butterfinger BB's/Bunch A Crunch Sidekick and Floorstand

DIVISION:

Temporary

SUB-CAT:

Candy, Gum and Mints

CLIENT:

Nestlé

ENTRANT:

Alliance Display & Packaging Corp.
Winston-Salem, NC

AWARD:

Bronze

TITLE:

Brach's 2' Snack Collection Display

DIVISION:

Permanent

SUB-CAT:

Candy, Gum and Mints

CLIENT:

E.J. Brach Corp.

ENTRANT:

Chicago Show
Morton Grove, IL

AWARD:

Bronze

TITLE:

Ultra Cooler Ice Barrel

DIVISION:

Temporary

SUB-CAT:

Soft Drinks, Mineral Waters and Powdered Mixes

CLIENT:

Pepsi Cola Co.

ENTRANT:

Display Technologies
Long Island City, NY

AWARD:

Bronze

TITLE:

Eveready Miniature Battery Display MIN-16IL

DIVISION:

Permanent

SUB-CAT:

Film and Batteries

CLIENT:

Eveready Battery Co., Inc.

ENTRANT:

Goldring Display Group, Inc.
Paramus, NJ

AWARD:

Bronze

TITLE:

20 and 52 Club Metalwood Displays

DIVISION:

Permanent

SUB-CAT:

Sports Equipment

CLIENT:

Taylor Made Golf Co.

ENTRANT:

Chicago Display Co.
Melrose Park, IL

AWARD:

Bronze

TITLE:

Fuji Quicksnap Camera Merchandiser

DIVISION:

Permanent

SUB-CAT:

Film and Batteries

CLIENT:

Fuji Photo Film Canada, Inc.

ENTRANT:

Admark Display, Ltd.
Scarborough, ONT, Canada

AWARD:

Gold

Fuji Photo Film Canada wanted a display that could hold a complete line of Quicksnap disposable cameras. The display also had to convey information to the consumer on the ease of use of the camera. The display had to be used as either a floor or counter unit. The display ultimately had to be attention getting.

Admark Display, Scarborough, ONT, Canada, used M.D.F. board, wire and metal, plastic extrusions, silk screening and litho graphics, turn tables, and a spun metal base on a floor stand to create the display. The display was designed for one year of use, had a production run of 1,200, and cost between $50 and $100 for the counter unit, $100 to $250 for the floor unit.

The display held 17 pounds of products and was shipped pre-packed. The display could be viewed from all four sides and rotated. Changeable panels were incorporated into the display for tie-in with media campaigns.

TITLE:

Pleasant Company Permanent Book Display

DIVISION:

Permanent

SUB-CAT:

Books and Games

CLIENT:

Pleasant Co.

ENTRANT:

**Great Northern Corp.,
Display Group
Racine, WI**

AWARD:

Silver

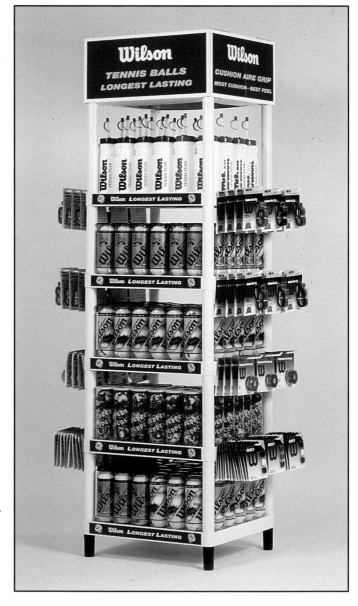

TITLE:

Wilson Spotlighter 2

DIVISION:

Permanent

SUB-CAT:

Sports Equipment

CLIENT:

Wilson Racquet Sports USA

ENTRANT:

**Mead Merchandising
Atlanta, GA**

AWARD:

Bronze

TITLE:

Lee Canter Resource Center

DIVISION:

Permanent

SUB-CAT:

Books and Games

CLIENT:

Lee Canter & Associates

ENTRANT:

R.P. Creative Sales, Inc.
Burbank, CA

AWARD:

Bronze

TITLE:

Unicorn Dart Center

DIVISION:

Permanent

SUB-CAT:

Sports Equipment

CLIENT:

General Sportcraft Co., Ltd.

ENTRANT:

R.E.A. Display, Inc.
Fairfield, NJ

AWARD:

Bronze

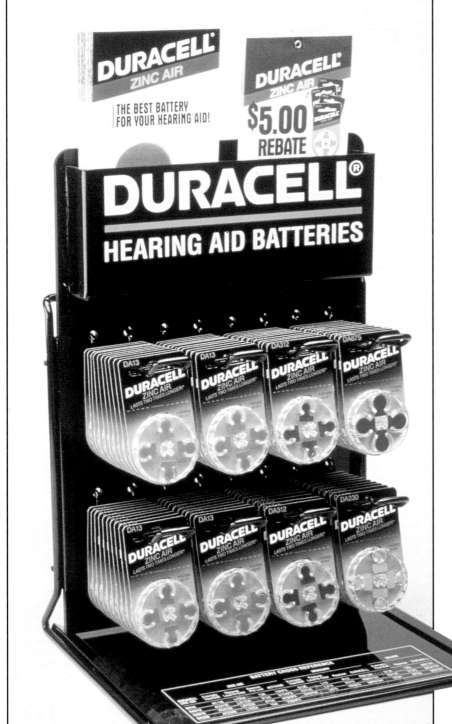

TITLE:
HA-D (Hearing Aid Display)
DIVISION:
Permanent
SUB-CAT:
Film and Batteries
CLIENT:
Duracell, Inc.
ENTRANT:
Display Creations, Inc.
Brooklyn, NY
AWARD:
Gold

Duracel had four major goals with the HA-D display. They were to provide a modular unit that could convert from eight SKU's to four SKU's for smaller retailers; eliminate assembly but still be sturdy and visible; provide consumers with visible permanent cross reference; and provide space within the display for consumer literature.

Display Creations, Brooklyn, NY, constructed a display of 3/16 and 1/8 black lucite, silk screening in two colors, and No. 4 steel wire with channels welded to a powder-coated black frame. The display could be used alone or on a peg board for an in-line display.

The display cost between $15 and $25 per unit to construct with 1,000 produced. It was intended to be used for a period of two years.

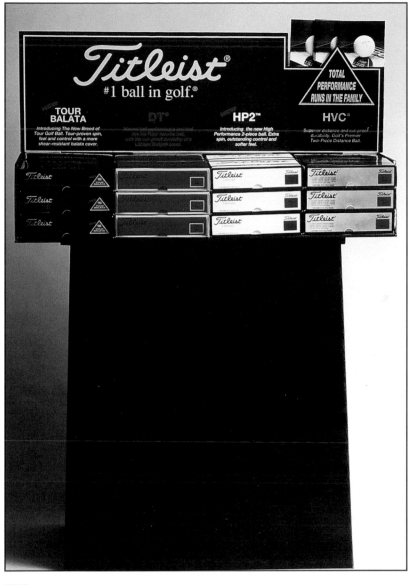

TITLE:

Titleist 24 Dozen Family Merchandiser

DIVISION:

Temporary

SUB-CAT:

Sports Equipment

ENTRANT:

**Titleist and Foot-Joy Worldwide
Fairhaven, MA**

AWARD:

Silver

TITLE:

Aerospace Jordan Floor Display

DIVISION:

Temporary

SUB-CAT:

Books and Games

CLIENT:

Nike, Inc.

ENTRANT:

**Rapid Mounting and Finishing Co.,
California Division
Union City, CA**

AWARD:

Bronze

TITLE:
Hogan Golf Ball/Glove Display

DIVISION:
Permanent

SUB-CAT:
Sports Equipment

CLIENT:
Ben Hogan Co.

ENTRANT:
**Robert Nielsen & Associates, Ltd.
Rolling Meadows, IL**

AWARD:
Silver

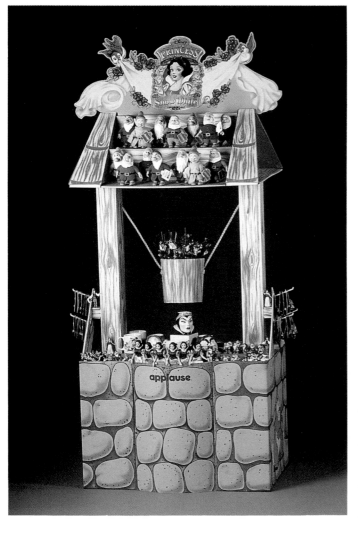

TITLE:
Snow White Floor Merchandiser

DIVISION:
Temporary

SUB-CAT:
Toys

CLIENT:
Applause, Inc.

ENTRANT:
**Applause, Inc.
Woodland Hills, CA**

AWARD:
Bronze

TITLE:
World of Enchantment Feature Display

DIVISION:
Temporary

SUB-CAT:
Books and Games

CLIENT:
Western Publishing Co., Inc.

ENTRANT:
**Chesapeake Display & Packaging Co.
Winston-Salem, NC**

AWARD:
Silver

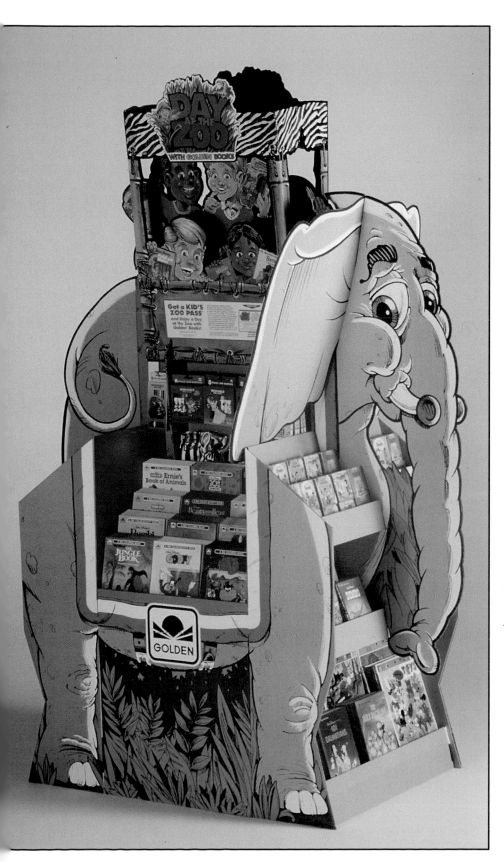

TITLE:

Golden Book Elephant Display

DIVISION:

Temporary

SUB-CAT:

Books and Games

CLIENT:

Western Publishing Co., Inc.

ENTRANT:

**Great Northern Corp.,
Display Group
Racine, WI**

AWARD:

Gold

*Free admission to the zoo was offered by Western
Publishing Company with the purchase of a Golden
Book. A display was needed to communicate the offer
and tie it in with the books being sold. Great Northern,
Racine, WI, created the display that could hold 1,200
pieces and communicate the special promotion.*

*The display, constructed of flexographic printed B-
flute corrugated, plastic clip and adapters, and litho
mounted corrugated, could hold 400 pounds of products,
and took only a four-foot square area. It was designed to
be used for a six- to eight-week period and had a
production run of 2,400. The display cost between $50
and $100 to construct.*

TITLE:

Jurassic Park

DIVISION:

Temporary

SUB-CAT:

Books and Games

CLIENT:

Western Publishing Co.

ENTRANT:

**Stone Container Corp.
Richmond, VA**

AWARD:

Silver

TITLE:

Snow White And The Seven Dwarfs

DIVISION:

Temporary

SUB-CAT:

Books and Games

CLIENT:

Western Publishing Co.

ENTRANT:

**Stone Container Corp.
Richmond, VA**

AWARD:

Silver

TITLE:
Lego Expandable/Retractable Valance System

DIVISION:
Permanent

SUB-CAT:
Toys

CLIENT:
Lego Systems, Inc.

ENTRANT:
**Thomas A. Schutz Co.,
Eastern Division
Westport, CT**

AWARD:
Silver

TITLE:
Marsupilami Floor Merchandiser

DIVISION:
Temporary

SUB-CAT:
Toys

CLIENT:
Applause, Inc.

ENTRANT:
**Applause, Inc.
Woodland Hills, CA**

AWARD:
Bronze

TITLE:
Toby Terrier Interactive Display

DIVISION:
Permanent

SUB-CAT:
Toys

CLIENT:
Tiger Electonics, Inc.

ENTRANT:
**RTC Industries, Inc.
Chicago, IL**

AWARD:
Silver

TITLE:
Easter Board Book Counter Display

DIVISION:
Temporary

SUB-CAT:
Books and Games

CLIENT:
Scholastic, Inc.

ENTRANT:
**Al Gar/The Display Connection, Inc.
Clifton, NJ**

AWARD:
Bronze

TITLE:
Aladdin Floor Merchandiser

DIVISION:
Temporary

SUB-CAT:
Toys

CLIENT:
Applause, Inc.

ENTRANT:
Applause, Inc.
Woodland Hills, CA

AWARD:
Gold

Applause, Inc., Woodland Hills, CA, created a display that was visually exciting to display the company's line of Disney products from the movie "Aladdin." The display utilized the Sultan's palace as the base structure and created an instant recognition. The display was engineered to appeal to the younger audience. Items that would appeal to younger children were placed at the bottom while items that would attract older children and teens were place farther up.

Constructed of litho sheets mounted to corrugated for the bottom, silk screening corrugated for the center, and tower section constructed of litho BSK, 4,400 of the units were produced. It cost between $25 and $50 per unit and was intended to be used for a period of four to six weeks.

TITLE:

"One Stop Wrap — Your Pillar Of Profits"

DIVISION:

Permanent

SUB-CAT:

Stationery, Party Goods, Giftwrap, Disposable Writing Instruments and Seasonal Items

CLIENT:

American Greetings Co.

ENTRANT:

**AG Industries,
American Greetings Corp.
Cleveland, OH**

AWARD:

Silver

TITLE:

Mother's Day Floor Merchandiser

DIVISION:

Temporary

SUB-CAT:

Stationery, Party Goods, Giftwrap, Disposable Writing Instruments and Seasonal Items

CLIENT:

Applause, Inc.

ENTRANT:

**Applause, Inc.
Woodland Hills, CA**

AWARD:

Silver

TITLE:

Winsor & Newton Carded Brush Module Display System

DIVISION:

Permanent

SUB-CAT:

Stationery, Party Goods, Giftwrap, Disposable Writing Instruments and Seasonal Items

CLIENT:

ColArt Americas, Inc.

ENTRANT:

**R.E.A. Display, Inc.
Fairfield, NJ**

AWARD:

Gold

ColArt America, Inc, wanted a display to merchandise a range of brushes that would assist customers in their decision. The display also had to be modular and be able to sit on a counter, hang on a wall or pegboard, or be used as a floorstand. It also had to allow retailers to be able to change prices with special "write-on wipe-off" strips, and provide retailers with bar code re-order information.

R.E.A. Displays, Fairfield, NJ, created the display using injection molded high impact polystyrene and glass filled polypropylene, gold hot stamped and metallized gold PVC extruded trim. The floorstand had painted medium density fiberboard, and metallized gold PVC extrusion. The counter unit had fabricated wire legs and the header was litho mounted.

The display was intended to be used for five years and 5,000 were produced. It cost between $100 and $250 to produce.

TITLE:

American Greetings CreataCard Corner

DIVISION:

Permanent

SUB-CAT:

Greeting Cards

CLIENT:

American Greetings Corp.

ENTRANT:

American Greetings Corp.
CreataCard
Cleveland, OH

AWARD:

Gold

American Greeting Corp., Cleveland, OH, developed a display that increased brand awareness via an interactive kiosk that allowed consumers to create their own individual cards. The display also triggered sales outside of the "normal" card shop areas.

A kiosk that had a three-sided design attracted and enticed customers to use it. The display's shell was constructed of wood, laminate and metal. An internal computer created the card. The kiosk was designed to be used for a period of five years and 103 displays were constructed. It cost over $1,000 per unit to build.

TITLE:

Keepsakes Gold Crown Merchandiser

DIVISION:

Permanent

SUB-CAT:

Stationery, Party Goods, Giftwrap, Disposable Writing Instruments and Seasonal Items

CLIENT:

Hallmark Cards, Inc.

ENTRANT:

**Hallmark Cards, Inc.
Kansas City, MO**

AWARD:

Silver

TITLE:

Trend Outpost

DIVISION:

Permanent

SUB-CAT:

Greeting Cards

CLIENT:

American Greetings Corp.

ENTRANT:

**American Greetings Corp.,
Calrton Cards, Inc.
Cleveland, OH**

AWARD:

Bronze

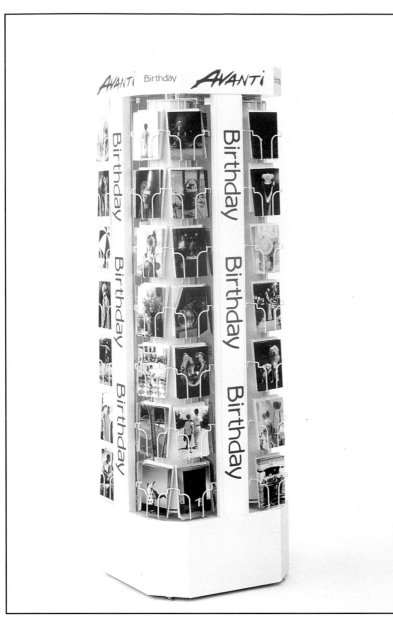

TITLE:
140 Pocket Greeting Card Merchandiser

DIVISION:
Permanent

SUB-CAT:
Greeting Cards

CLIENT:
Avanti

ENTRANT:
**Great Northern Corp.,
Display Group
Racine, WI**

AWARD:
Silver

TITLE:
U.S. Stamp Staples Program

DIVISION:
Permanent

SUB-CAT:
**Stationery, Party Goods, Giftwrap, Disposable Writing Instruments
and Seasonal Items**

CLIENT:
U.S. Stamp

ENTRANT:
**R.P. Creative Sales, Inc.
Burbank, CA**

AWARD:
Bronze

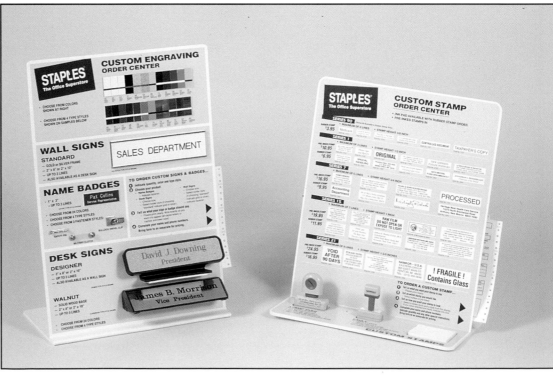

TITLE:
Enesco's Precious Moments Noah's Ark Display

DIVISION:
Permanent

SUB-CAT:
Stationery, Party Goods, Giftwrap, Disposable Writing Instruments and Seasonal Items

CLIENT:
Enesco Corp.

ENTRANT:
**United Packaging Co.
Schaumburg, IL**

AWARD:
Bronze

TITLE:
Up, Up & Away

DIVISION:
Temporary

SUB-CAT:
Stationery, Party Goods, Giftwrap, Disposable Writing Instruments and Seasonal Items

CLIENT:
American Greetings

ENTRANT:
**The Dyment Co.,
Cleveland Division
Cleveland, OH**

AWARD:
Bronze

Rock Island Displays, Milan, IL, created a display for Hallmark Cards, Inc., that would merchandise and attract customers to the Crayola line of juvenile gift wrap. The display would be used during best selling formats, especially during the back-to-school selling periods of the summer months. The display incorporated a coin bank that could be used when the wrapping paper was used up. The paper display had to promote the relationship between Hallmark/Ambassador and Binney & Smith, maker of the Crayola crayons.

The display utilized corrugated and printed letterpress with plastic trim. The display could be used as an endcap, and delivered a quick, clear, compelling message. Five thousand displays were made at a cost of $25 to $50 per display. It was intended to be used for an eight-week time period.

TITLE:
Crayola Gift Wrap Program

DIVISION:
Temporary

SUB-CAT:
Stationery, Party Goods, Giftwrap, Disposable Writing Instruments and Seasonal Items

CLIENT:
Hallmark Cards, Inc.

ENTRANT:
Rock Island Display
Milan, IL

AWARD:
Gold

TITLE:
Pilot / Spotliter Supreme Display

DIVISION:
Permanent

SUB-CAT:
Stationery, Party Goods, Giftwrap, Disposable Writing Instruments and Seasonal Items

CLIENT:
Pilot Pen Corp.

ENTRANT:
**Ultimate Display Industries, Inc.
Jamaica, NY**

AWARD:
Bronze

TITLE:
Micrographx Draw Floor Display

DIVISION:
Temporary

SUB-CAT:
Office Equipment and Supplies

CLIENT:
Micrografx

ENTRANT:
**Great Northern Corp.,
Display Group
Racine, WI**

AWARD:
Silver

TITLE:

Halloween Counter Displays

DIVISION:

Temporary

SUB-CAT:

Stationery, Party Goods, Giftwrap, Disposable Writing Instruments and Seasonal Items

CLIENT:

Applause, Inc.

ENTRANT:

Applause, Inc.
Woodland Hills, CA

AWARD:

Silver

TITLE:

Frankie's Castle

DIVISION:

Temporary

SUB-CAT:

Stationery, Party Goods, Giftwrap, Disposable Writing Instruments and Seasonal Items

CLIENT:

American Greetings Corp.

ENTRANT:

The Dyment Co.,
Cleveland Division
Cleveland, OH

AWARD:

Silver

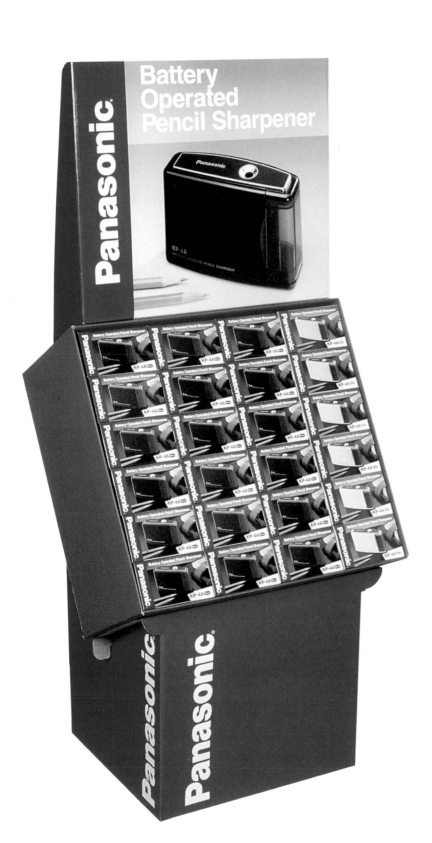

TITLE:
Panasonic Pencil Sharpener

DIVISION:
Temporary

SUB-CAT:
Office Equipment and Supplies

CLIENT:
Panasonic

ENTRANT:
Frank Mayer & Associates, Inc.
Grafton, WI

AWARD:
Gold

The display for Panasonic's pencil sharpener had to present the product in a consumer friendly manner, in an environment that is usually crowded and cluttered. It also had to meet retailers' requirements for either pre-packs or store set-up displays. Frank Mayer & Associates, Inc., Grafton, WI, created the display utilizing corrugated.

The 1,300 displays made the product stand out in the retail environment. All items were packed neatly into one bin, making it easy to restock. Retailers were given the option to order the display as set up and pre-packs or as flat. The display could support up to 50 pounds of product.

The display was intended to be used for a two-month period at a cost of $50 to $100 per unit.

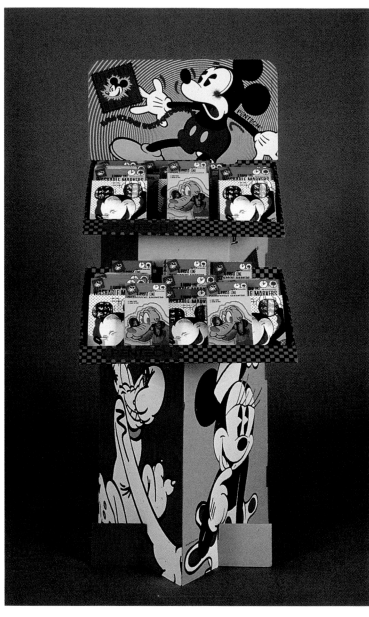

TITLE:

Pentech Disney

DIVISION:

Temporary

SUB-CAT:

**Stationery, Party Goods, Giftwrap, Disposable Writing Instruments
and Seasonal Items**

CLIENT:

Pentech International, Inc.

ENTRANT:

**McLean Packaging Corp.
Philadelphia, PA**

AWARD:

Bronze

TITLE:

Basic Party Merchandiser—Thanksgiving and Halloween

DIVISION:

Temporary

SUB-CAT:

**Stationery, Party Goods, Giftwrap, Disposable Writing Instruments
and Seasonal Items**

CLIENT:

Ambassador

ENTRANT:

**Chesapeake Display & Packaging,
Chesapeake Corp.
Winston-Salem, NC**

AWARD:

Bronze

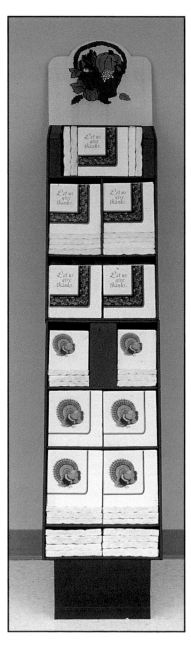

TITLE:

Santa's Workshop

DIVISION:

Temporary

SUB-CAT:

**Stationery, Party Goods, Giftwrap, Disposable Writing Instruments
and Seasonal Items**

CLIENT:

American Greetings Corp.

ENTRANT:

**The Dyment Co.,
Cleveland Division
Cleveland, OH**

AWARD:

Bronze

TITLE:
Philip Morris Marlboro Illuminated 2-Sided Clock

DIVISION:
Permanent

SUB-CAT:
Cigarettes - Illuminated

CLIENT:
Philip Morris USA

ENTRANT:
**Process Displays, Inc.
New Berlin, WI**

AWARD:
Silver

TITLE:
Marlboro Exterior Signage Program

DIVISION:
Permanent

SUB-CAT:
Cigarettes - Non-Illuminated

CLIENT:
Philip Morris U.S.A.

ENTRANT:
**Thomson-Leeds Co., Inc.
New York, NY**

AWARD:
Gold

Thomson-Leeds Co., New York, NY, developed a signage program for Philip Morris USA to be used in gasoline stations, convenience stores, and other shopping areas where cigarettes are sold. The program had to flag passing customers and deliver the message that Marlboro cigarettes were sold in that location. The signage program had to be designed so it would be placed in a special desirable location and guarantee long term placement.

Silk screened aluminum, wire and metal tubing were utilized to create the program. Rounded corners made the displays appear contemporary. The program also utilized durable exterior finishes and weather-resistant products. Units were shipped completely assembled and required only the legs to be attached.

The program was designed to be used for several years and over 100,000 were constructed. The display cost between $100 to $250 to construct. The signs have been placed in high traffic areas throughout the United States and have been extremely successful.

A display that was going to be used in newspaper stands, drug stores, convenience stores and other retail outlets that sell lottery tickets was needed. Philip Morris wanted a display that could be used in these locations and tie-in the popular lotto theme. The displays would promote Marlboro brands and also convey information on jackpot sizes and winning numbers.

Thomson-Leeds Co., New York, NY, created a display that had a 3-D effect. A new jumping horse graphic was used on the two-sided display. The display had a dry erase bottom section so that jackpot amounts and winning numbers could be displayed.

Constructed of injection molded styrene, hot stamping, lithography, sheet lamination, plastic and metal hardware, 12,000 of the display were manufactured. The display cost between $10 and $15 per unit to construct and was to be used for a one-year period.

TITLE:

Marlboro Lotto Sign

DIVISION:

Permanent

SUB-CAT:

Cigarettes - Non-Illuminated

CLIENT:

Philip Morris U.S.A.

ENTRANT:

**Thomson-Leeds Co., Inc.
New York, NY**

AWARD:

Gold

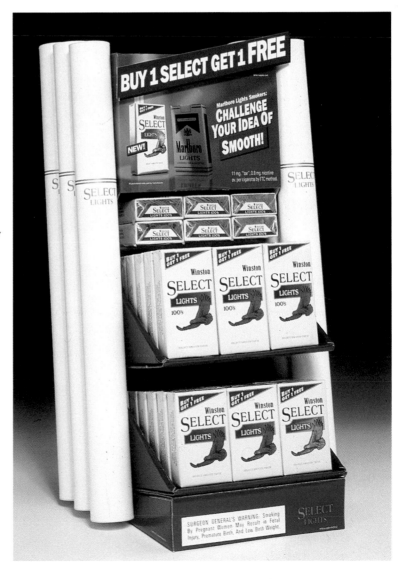

TITLE:

Winston Select Lights Counter Display

DIVISION:

Temporary

SUB-CAT:

Cigarettes - Non-Illuminated

CLIENT:

R.J. Reynolds Tobacco Co.

ENTRANT:

**Chesapeake Display & Packaging Co.
Winston-Salem, NC**

AWARD:

Silver

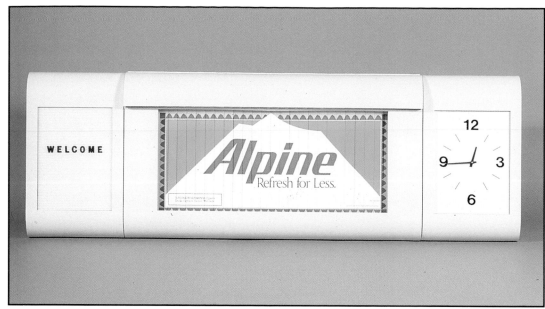

TITLE:
Tri Vision Moveable Sign

DIVISION:
Permanent

SUB-CAT:
Cigarettes - Illuminated

CLIENT:
Philip Morris U.S.A.

ENTRANT:
**Thomson-Leeds Co., Inc.
New York, NY**

AWARD:
Silver

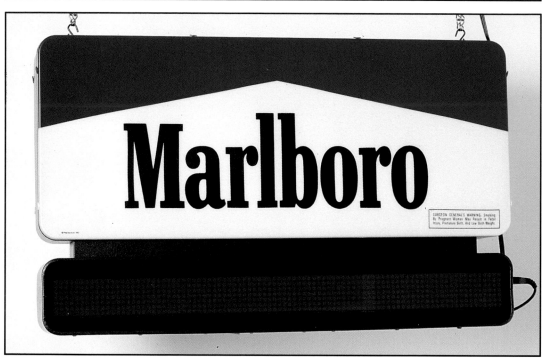

TITLE:
Marlboro Illuminated L.E.D. Sign

DIVISION:
Permanent

SUB-CAT:
Cigarettes - Illuminated

CLIENT:
Philip Morris U.S.A.

Entrant:
**Thomson-Leeds Co., Inc.
New York, NY**

AWARD:
Bronze

TITLE:
Parliament Wave Clock Sign

DIVISION:
Permanent

SUB-CAT:
Cigarettes - Illuminated

CLIENT:
Philip Morris, U.S.A.

ENTRANT:
**Thomson-Leeds Co., Inc.
New York, NY**

AWARD:
Bronze

TITLE:

R.J. Reynolds Integrated Check-Out Counter Merchandiser

DIVISION:

Permanent

SUB-CAT:

Cigarettes - Illuminated

CLIENT:

R.J. Reynolds Tobacco Co.

ENTRANT:

Eddy Associates, Inc.
New Berlin, WI
Rep.: Storewars - Phoenix, AZ

AWARD:

Gold

Eddy Associates, New Berlin, WI, created an entire check-out system for R.J. Reynolds Tobacco Company to be used in Circle-K convenience stores. The system had to promote Reynolds brands awareness and ultimately increase sales. The system was placed in 2,600 stores and was intended to stay in place for seven to ten years.

When in place, the system appeared to give stores a remodeled look. It was cleaner and decreased counter clutter. By allowing space for a second cash register, speed of check-out was increased. The lighted counter system greatly improved store image and sales on cigarette package sales, and promotional items increased as well.

Fabricated wood, fabricated wire, vacuum formed styrene and extruded vinyl was used in the construction of the counter system. The display was tied-in with Circle K television ads promoting the "new look" of the stores. It cost over $1,000 per system to construct.

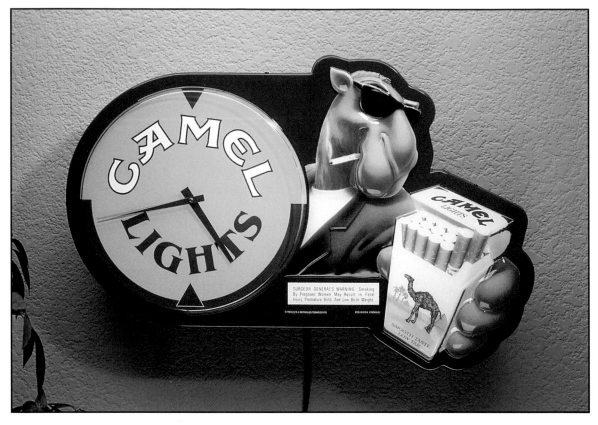

TITLE:
Camel Lighted Clock

DIVISION:
Permanent

SUB-CAT:
Cigarettes - Illuminated

CLIENT:
R.J. Reynolds Tocacco Co.

ENTRANT:
**KCS Industries, Inc.,
A Banta Corp. Subsidiary
Milwaukee, WI**

AWARD:
Silver

TITLE:
High Impact Semi-Permanent Counter Display

DIVISION:
Permanent

SUB-CAT:
Cigarettes - Non-Illuminated

CLIENT:
R.J. Reynolds Tobacco Co.

ENTRANT:
**Decision Point Marketing
Winston-Salem, NC**

AWARD:
Silver

TITLE:

2' Gristedes Overhead Pack Merchandiser

DIVISION:

Permanent

SUB-CAT:

Cigarettes - Non-Illuminated

CLIENT:

Philip Morris U.S.A.

ENTRANT:

**Henschel-Steinau, Inc.
Englewood, NJ**

AWARD:

Silver

TITLE:

Winston Weekends Catalogue - Floorbase and Counter Displays

DIVISION:

Temporary

SUB-CAT:

Cigarettes - Non-Illuminated

CLIENT:

R.J. Reynolds Tobacco Co.

ENTRANT:

**Chesapeake Display & Packaging Co.
Winston-Salem, NC**

AWARD:

Bronze

TITLE:
Marlboro "Billy" Floor Ashtray

DIVISION:
Permanent

SUB-CAT:
Cigarettes - Non-Illuminated

CLIENT:
Philip Morris U.S.A.

ENTRANT:
**Henschel-Steinau, Inc.
Englewood, NJ**

AWARD:
Bronze

TITLE:
Marlboro Billy Flag System

DIVISION:
Temporary

SUB-CAT:
Cigarettes - Non-Illuminated

CLIENT:
Philip Morris U.S.A.

ENTRANT:
**Thomson-Leeds Co., Inc.
New York, NY**

AWARD:
Silver

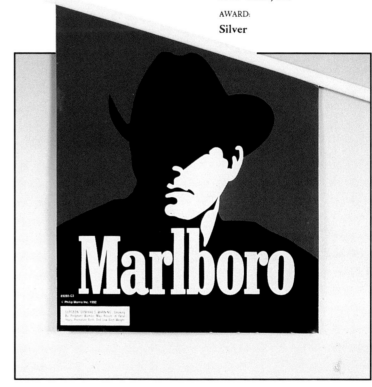

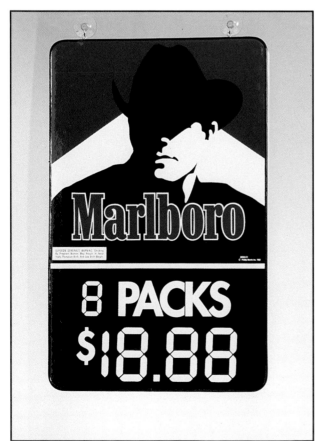

TITLE:
Marlboro Billy Pricing Sign

DIVISION:
Temporary

SUB-CAT:
Cigarettes - Non-Illuminated

CLIENT:
Philip Morris U.S.A.

ENTRANT:
**Thomson-Leeds Co., Inc.
New York, NY**

AWARD:
Silver

TITLE:

R.J. Reynolds Tobacco Universal Decor Program

DIVISION:

Permanent

SUB-CAT:

Cigarettes - Non-Illuminated

CLIENT:

R.J. Reynolds Tobacco Co.

ENTRANT:

Thomas A. Schutz Co., Inc.
Morton Grove, IL

AWARD:

Silver

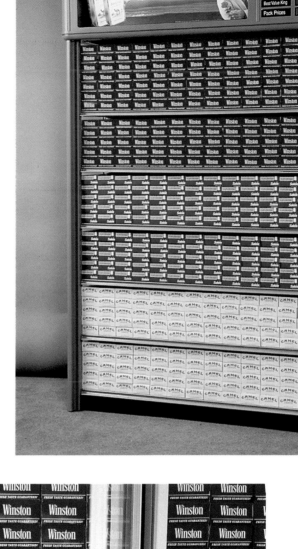

TITLE:

Remote Solid Door Locking System

DIVISION:

Permanent

SUB-CAT:

Cigarettes - Illuminated

CLIENT:

R.J. Reynolds Tobacco Co.

ENTRANT:

Intermark (The Howard Marlboro Group)
New York, NY

AWARD:

Bronze

TITLE:
R.J. Reynolds Magnalite Program

DIVISION:
Permanent

SUB-CAT:
Cigarettes - Illuminated

CLIENT:
R.J. Reynolds Tobacco Co.

ENTRANT:
**Thomas A. Schutz Co., Inc.
Motron Grove, IL**

AWARD:
Bronze

TITLE:
R. J. Reynolds "1/2 Y" Program

DIVISION:
Permanent

SUB-CAT:
Cigarettes - Illuminated

CLIENT:
R.J. Reynolds Tobacco Co.

ENTRANT:
**Visual Marketing, Inc.
Chicago, IL**

AWARD:
Bronze

TITLE:
Camel "Special Lights" Louvre Motion

DIVISION:
Temporary

SUB-CAT:
Cigarettes - Non-Illuminated

CLIENT:
R.J. Reynolds Tobacco Company

ENTRANT:
Lemmond and Associates
Charlotte, NC

AWARD:
Gold

A low-cost, high impact advertising display was needed to establish brand awareness and encourage trial on the new Camel Special Lights cigarettes by R.J. Reynolds Tobacco. The display had to adhere to the top of a permanent promotional display, and on or near the cash register.

Lemmond and Associates, Charlotte, NC, constructed a display of lithography, mounting and finishing, and a D.C. motor with batteries. The display had a motion louvre that allowed the display to constantly change between two different messages.

The display was designed to be used for a period of three to six months, and 11,000 were made. The cost to construct was between $25 and $50 per unit.

TITLE:
Parliament Counter Change Tray

DIVISION:
Permanent

SUB-CAT:
Cigarettes - Non-Illuminated

CLIENT:
Philip Morris U.S.A.

ENTRANT:
Thomson-Leeds Co., Inc.
New York, NY

AWARD:
Bronze

TITLE:
Kmart Car Stereo Switching Display

DIVISION:
Permanent

SUB-CAT:
Automotive Aftermarket

CLIENT:
Kmart Corp.

ENTRANT:
**DCI Marketing
Milwaukee, WI**

AWARD:
Gold

Kmart wanted a switching display that eliminated the $600,000 annual service contract and allowed store personnel to make all future stereo component change-outs. The display also had to represent the company's new upscale look and provide equal presentations of the participating car stereo vendors. It also had to be salesperson friendly and informative.

DCI Marketing, Milwaukee, WI, developed the display as a modular unit to control costs. Individual component sizes were evaluated to develop cutout sizes. The display had the company's new look via color-matched ABS and conformed to the store's expansion and renovations projects.

It was constructed of color-matched ABS vacuum formed one-piece shell over vinyl-clad particle board housing, with automotive accent trim. The display was meant to be used for five years and 2,300 will eventually be placed in Kmart stores. The cost of the display was over $1,000 per display.

TITLE:

1993 Isuzu Product Reference Guide

DIVISION:

Permanent

SUB-CAT:

Passenger Cars and Specialty Vehicles

CLIENT:

American Isuzu Motors, Inc.

ENTRANT:

DCI Marketing
Milwaukee, WI

AWARD:

Bronze

TITLE:

Cadillac DeVille/DeVille Concours Promotion

DIVISION:

Permanent

SUB-CAT:

Passenger Cars and Specialty Vehicles

CLIENT:

General Motors Corp.

ENTRANT:

DCI Marketing
Milwaukee, WI

AWARD:

Silver

TITLE:
Ford Motor Credit - Credit Information System

DIVISION:
Permanent

SUB-CAT:
Passenger Cars and Specialty Vehicles

CLIENT:
Ford Motor Credit

ENTRANT:
**AG Industries,
American Greetings Corp.
Cleveland, OH**

AWARD:
Silver

TITLE:
Gabriel Program 1993

DIVISION:
Permanent

SUB-CAT:
Automotive Aftermarket

CLIENT:
Gabriel Ride Control Products

ENTRANT:
**Thomas A. Schutz Co., Inc.
Morton Grove, IL**

AWARD:
Bronze

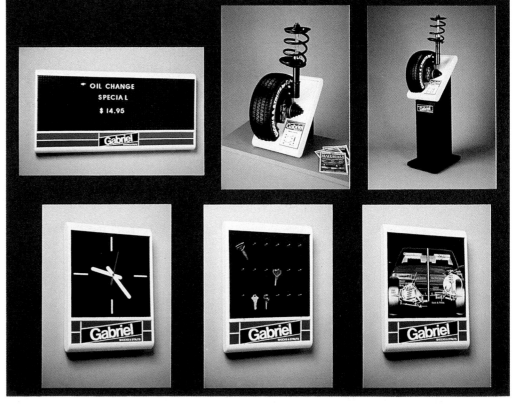

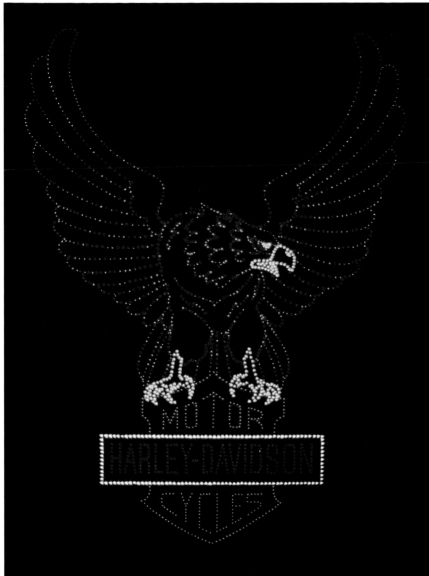

TITLE:
Harley Davidson Fiber Optic Display

DIVISION:
Permanent

SUB-CAT:
Passenger Cars and Specialty Vehicles

CLIENT:
Harley-Davidson, Inc.

ENTRANT:
Fiberoptic Lighting, Inc.
Grants Pass, OR

AWARD:
Gold

Harley-Davidson wanted to expose more customers to their many faceted product line besides motorcycles. Fiberoptic Lighting, Inc., Grants Pass, OR, created a display that could attract attention from a distance, but up close had a quieter impact and allowed the merchandise to be the focal point.

Using a birch plywood cabinet with plastic laminate, ABS plastic face, silk screened acrylic color encoded discs, halogen lamps, synchronized motors and acrylic fiber optic strands, the displays were constructed. The displays would be used for a period of five years at a cost of over $1,000 per display. It also was pictured occasionally in its environment for magazine ads.

TITLE:
Safe-Lode Ground Access Sign

DIVISION:
Permanent

SUB-CAT:
Petroleum Products

CLIENT:
Diamond Shamrock Refining &Mktg

ENTRANT:
Arlington Aluminum Co.
Detroit, MI

AWARD:
Silver

TITLE:
Cadillac Leasing Car Topper

DIVISION:
Permanent

SUB-CAT:
Passenger Cars and Specialty Vehicles

CLIENT:
General Motors Corp.

ENTRANT:
DCI Marketing
Milwaukee, WI

AWARD:
Bronze

TITLE:
Dorman Gatefold System

DIVISION:
Permanent

SUB-CAT:
Automotive Aftermarket

CLIENT:
Dorman Products, Inc.

ENTRANT:
Tusco Display
Gnadenhutten, OH

AWARD:
Bronze

TITLE:
Kelly-Springfield Light Truck Tire Display

DIVISION:
Permanent

SUB-CAT:
Automotive Aftermarket

CLIENT:
Kelly-Springfield Tire Co.

ENTRANT:
Frank Mayer & Associates, Inc.
Grafton, WI

AWARD:
Silver

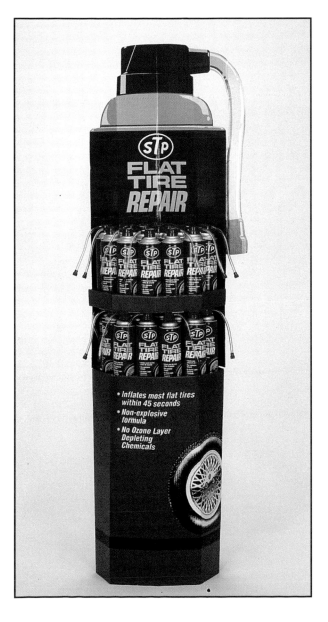

TITLE:
STP Flat Tire Repair

DIVISION:
Temporary

SUB-CAT:
Automotive Aftermarket

CLIENT:
First Brands

ENTRANT:
Stone Container Corp.
Richmond, VA

AWARD:
Bronze

Anheuser-Busch, Inc. Selected as POPAI's 1993 Chief Award Winner

PHOTO BY HARVARD STUDIO

The Point-of-Purchase Advertising Institute (POPAI), Englewood, NJ, awarded the prestigious Chief Award, which recognizes merchandising excellence in point-of-purchase advertising, to Anheuser-Busch, Inc. Richard Nathan, POPAI Chairman of the Board and President, RTC Industries, Inc., makes the presentation to Patrick T. Stokes, President, Anheuser-Busch, Inc. Left to right: Dick Blatt, POPAI Executive Director; Don Ferguson, POPAI First Vice Chairman and President Gor-Don Metal Products; Scott Murdock, Group Director Merchandising and Promotions Development, Anheuser-Busch, Inc.; Stokes, Nathan, Chuck Koenig, Director of Corporate Purchasing, Anheuser-Busch, Inc.; Doug Leeds, POPAI Marketplace '93 Chairman and President, Thomson-Leeds; and Dick Fellinger, POPAI Treasurer, and President, Mechtronics.

The Point of Purchase Advertising Institute (POPAI) presented its Chief Award for merchandising excellence to Anheuser-Busch, Inc., at the POPAI Chief Award Dinner at New York's Marriott Marquis Hotel. The event took place during POPAI's Marketplace '93, the world's largest in-store advertising show, which was held at the Jacob Javits Convention Center.

"We are truly honored this year to present the Chief Award to such a P-O-P industry pioneer," said Richard Nathan, POPAI Chairman of the Board. "Anheuser-Busch is a company that has dedicated itself to innovative in-store designs that have consistently merited recognition from the POPAI Outstanding Merchandising Achievement (OMA) Awards competition."

Patrick T. Stokes, President, Anheuser-Busch, Inc., accepted the prestigious award. The evening honoring Anheuser-Busch, Inc., the world's largest brewer and industry leader in the United States since 1957, included entertainment by the internationally acclaimed musical legend Ray Charles and his orchestra.

The Chief Award recipient is selected annually by a blue-ribbon panel representing all segments of POPAI membership. The award itself is the highest honor bestowed by POPAI upon a consumer product manufacturer or retailer. Recipients must have contributed to the advancement of point-of-purchase advertising through demonstrated and consistent use of P-O-P and general support of the industry. They must also have consistently observed ethical practices in dealing the P-O-P producers/suppliers and in its general business practices.

Past recipients of POPAI's Chief Award include: Nintendo of America Inc.; General Motors Corporation; Warner-Lambert Company; McDonald's Corporation; Procter & Gamble Company; Philip Morris Companies; Coca-Cola Company; Hallmark Cards, Inc.; and the R.J. Reynolds Tobacco Company.

David Abbruzzese
Nabisco Foods Group

Gunter Alberts
Florsheim Shoe Company

Greg Allen
The Bonneau Companies

Jacqueline Allen
The Southland Corporation

Sue Altschul
Philip Morris U.S.A.

Sharon Amelio
United States Tobacco Company

Kimberly Anderson
Letraset, Division of Esselte Pendaflex

Sheila Anderson
Mattel Toys

Kathy Antoniades
Planters LifeSavers Company

Michael A. Arecchi
Revlon, Incorporated

Richard W. Arent
Kimberly-Clark Corporation

Marti Baer
Applause Incorporated

David R. Baranowski
Anheuser-Busch Companies, Inc.

Camille Barkley
Random House Incorporated

Steve Bartolucci
The Gillette Company/Stationery
Products

Robert A. Bednar
Matrix Essentials, Incorporated

Brenda Bell
Procter & Gamble Cosmetics &
Fragrances

Peter P. Berardino
American Express TRS Company,
Incorporated

John E. Berkheimer
Anheuser-Busch Companies, Inc.

Robert N. Bernstein
House of Seagram

Richard Betsch
The Procter & Gamble Company

Arthur Birn
Schwarz Paper Company

Peter Q. Bishop
Benjamin Moore & Company

Jeffrey Bisson
Caldor Incorporated

David Blumenthal
Lion Brand Yarn Company

Samuel L. Bonacci
Hershey International

Charles Boulter
The Southland Corporation

Howard Brauner
Magnivision

Barry Brewer
Loctite Corporation

Robert G. Brisky
The Glidden Company Division of ICI
Paints

Dar Britzman
Nestle Food Company

Ted Brolsma
GenCorp Polymer Products

Lauren Brown
Calvin Klein Cosmetics

Nancy M. Bruner
Kraft USA

Susan Burdette
Miller Brewing Company

John P. Burns
Tarkett, Incorporated

Laurie Burns
The Quaker Oats Company

Mark E. Bush
Heinz, USA

Patricia Byer
Estee Lauder

Jerry Cahee
Warner Press Incorporated

Gene Cairo
KLIC

Lorraine Caldwell
Heublein, Incorporated

James A. Cantela
Elizabeth Arden Company

Joanne M. Cardello
Perscriptives International

Lisa Caroll
Tsumura International

Greg Casey
Nintendo of America Inc.

Meg Casey
Heublein, Incorporated (Hart Division)

Marva Cathey
The Southland Corporation

Mark Channing
Channing Merchandising Corporation

Lily A. Chow
American Express TRS Company,
Incorporated

Michael E. Christen
Herff Jones, Incorporated

Anita Clark
Johnson Controls

Michael Cohen
Sony Electronics

Gail Cohen
Go Lightly Candy Company Incorporated

Lynn B. Columbus
Enesco Corporation

Adrienne J. Coppola
MEM Company, Incorporated

Louise Cote
Allied-Signal Incorporated/Automotive
Aftermarket

Robert H. Crawford III
R.J. Reynolds Tobacco Company

Andrea Crouch
Chattem Consumer Products

Susan Curatola
Sterling Health Incorporated

Del D'Lower
Delby System

Violette Daabous
Hiram Walker & Sons Incorporated

Max E. Damron
The Procter & Gamble Company

Ila Dane
Live Home Video

Ann O. Danner
Anheuser-Busch, Incorporated

Gino De Luca
Gillette Canada Incorporated

Christopher J. DeMarco
Duracell, U.S.A.

Camille DeRose
Gibson-Homans Company

John J. Dean, III
R.J. Reynolds Tobacco Company

David Noble Dittmann
Thayers Apothecary Company

Gary D. Donatell
Honeywell, Incorporated

Christopher D. Donnelly
Allied Signal-Fram Filters

Leanne Douglass
Webway, Incorporated

Jim Drawbridge
Nabisco Brands, Incorporated

J. Jerome Dudley
The Procter & Gamble
Cosmetic & Fragrance Products

Robert C. Dyer
Thrift Drug, Incorporated

Allan T. Falvey
Warner Lambert-Consumer Health

Steven M. Feigenbaum
MEM Company, Incorporated

Michael V. Feldmann
First Colony Coffee & Tea Company

Todd Ferguson
Toyota Motor Sales, USA

Terri Ferrell
Schering-Plough Healthcare Products,
Incorporated

Michael P. Finnegan
Chattem Consumer Products

Stephen Flusser
Aris Isotoner

David Foreman
Guiltless Gourmet, Incorporated

Denise Friscia
L'Oreal Salon Products

Sandra M. Gallo
Miller Brewing Company

Lawrence J. Gazlay
General Sportcraft Company, Limited

Richard Gellis
Polaroid Corporation

James D. George
Hershey Chocolate USA

Arlene Gerwin
Heublein

Michael Gianino
Anheuser-Busch, Incorporated

John Gilbertie
Tambrands, Incorporated

Bob Giraldi
Nike, Incorporated

Thomas Glynn
Schieffelin & Somerset Company

Wendy Gordon
The HB Group

Michael J. Goshko
Amoco Corporation

Ed Gove
Hartley Gove Sons

Julie A. Graham
Coca-Cola USA

Vickie Graham
Hallmark Cards, Incorporated

Thomas Granville
Anheuser-Busch, Incorporated

Jan E. Graveline
Johnson Controls, Incorporated

Robert Lee Gray
The Goodyear Tire & Rubber Company

Glenna Greene
Coca-Cola USA

Neil Guller
Conair Corporation

Charles Haberkorn
Pepperidge Farm

Chuck Hardinger
Miller Brewing Company

Beverly C. Harlan
Riceland Foods, Incorporated

Jay Hawkinson
The Dial Corporation

Kevin M. Healy
Titleist and Foot-Joy Worldwide

Janet Healy
Rust-Oleum Corporation

Dan Hedrick
Brown-Forman Beverage Company-
Jack Daniels

Ken B. Hedrick
R.J. Reynolds Tobacco Company

Karen Herman
Random House

Lisa Herman
Castrol Incorporated

Richard Lee Hilton
Dr. Pepper/Seven-Up Company,
Incorporated

Kelly Jo Hinrichs
Cliffs Notes, Incorporated

Shelly Hoffman
First Brand Corporation

Martha D. Hubbard
Maybelline, Incorporated

Joe Huesman
The Procter & Gamble Company

Douglas Huffmyer
Calvin Klein Cosmetics Company

Lee Huggins
Kayser-Roth Corporation

J. Paul Jasper
Consumer Health Care-Pfizer,
Incorporated

Scott Jennie
The Gibson-Homans Company

Mary Ellen Johnson
Frito-Lay

Craig Kalter
French Toast

Gerald Katz
Fay's, Incorporated

Brian Kelly
Eastman Kodak Company

Stephie Kirschner
Crystal Brands Jewelry Group

Richard J. Kirwin
Amity Leather Products Company

Bruce L. Kline
Pentapco.

David J. Kmetz
General Foods USA

Dennis A. Knaus
Stroh Brewery Company

Keith Kolakoski
Reckitt & Colman, Incorporated

Art Koon
American Chicle

Rudy Kral
M&M/Mars

Doug Kwikkel
Miller Brewing Company

Michael E. LaBroad
Anheuser-Busch, Inc.

Peter A. LaGuardia
The Equitable Life Assurance Society

Ron Lamb
Allied Signal, Incorporated

Dan Lammon
A.T. Cross, Incorporated

Michael J. Lanaghan
William Wrigley Jr. Company

Jane A. Langa
Anheuser-Busch, Inc.

Glynn LeBlanc
Bengal Chemical, Incorporated

Brian E. Little
Philip Morris USA

Jack Long
Chesco Corporation

James Long
Hallmark Cards, Incorporated

Tony Lorenzo
Cavanaugh Press, Incorporated

Thomas Lowry
Balkamp, Incorporated

Dennis Madigan
Miller Brewing Company

Andrea L. Martin
E. & J. Gallo Winery

Cecilia Martin
American Greetings

Liane May
Random House, Incorporated

Thomas E. Maynard
Eagle Electric Manufacturing
Company, Incorporated

James M. Mayor
Hearst Distribution Group

Brian X. McCormack
Warner-Lambert Company

Laura McCurry
Coca-Cola USA

RoseMary McDaniel
Miles, Incorporated

Kevin McGrath
James Galt Company, Incorporated

Susan M. McIver
AT&T

Jacqueline M. McLaurin
R.J. Reynolds Tobacco Company

Rosemary F. Milby
Scott Paper Company

Rebecca Miller
Specialty Brands

Meg Moedritzer
David Sherman Corporation

Ruth Monstvilas
Dana Perfumes

George Morandin
GSW Thermoplastics Company

Terry Morrissey
Black & Decker

Daniel Multer
Israel Ministiry of Tourism,
North America

Scott E. Murdock
Anheuser-Busch, Inc.

Robert Murphree
Maybelline, Incorporated

Calvin W. Myer
Worldwide Company/
McDonald's Corporation

Christine M. Nagy
Rothman's, Benson & Hedges,
Incorporated

Stanley G. Navyac
Hiram Walker & Sons, Incorporated

Susan L. Neumann
Applause, Incorporated

Rene Newman
Nestlé Chocolate & Confectionery
Company

David A. Nicholson
Revlon, Incorporated

Patricia Nilson
Simplicity Pattern Company

Mary Noller
Sandoz Consumer Pharmaceuticals

Lee Nordgren
Kayser-Roth Corporation

Tom Norman
Hershey Chocolate USA

Robert E. Norwick
Estee Lauder, Incorporated

Kenneth Noskin
Coty

Thomas O'Brien
Edwards Baking Company

Bill O'Hare
MacKlanburg-Duncan

R. Donald O'Leary
The Great Atlantic & Pacific Tea
Company

Kathi L. O'Neil
Hearst Magazines

Mike O'Sullivan
Anheuser-Busch, Inc.

Charlotte Oades
Coca-Cola USA

Steve Oliver
Exxon Company USA

Robert J. Passarelli
Ekco Housewares

Elizabeth Paulley
Brown & Williamson Tobacco

Martin M. Pegler
Fashion Institute of Technology NYC

H. Pierce Pelouze III
Campbell Soup Company

Chris Pfaus
S-B Power Tool Company

Peter C. Pfeil
The Procter & Gamble Company

Jan D. Podesva
Parfums de Coeur

C. Frank Potter
Mannington Resilient Floors

Michael K. Pukay
Imperial Wallcoverings

Joanne Purchase
Rosedale Wallcoverings

Sherry Raedel
Cadbury Beverages

Scott Rexinger
Leiner Health Products, Incorporated

Joseph T. Ricci
Duracell, U.S.A.

Fred Richman

John Riveroll
Just Born, Incorporated

Ted Roberts
Miller Brewing Company

Mary M. Rodgers
Faberware, Incorporated

JoLynn W. Rogers
Ideal Industries, Incorporated

Kay L. Roseland
Honeywell, Incorporated

George Rutkowski
Cooper Lighting

John A. Sakaley III
Nintendo of America Incorporated

Robert A. Santoli
Schieffelin & Somerset Company

Joseph A. Sbrocco
General Electric

John Scalfani
Warner-Lambert/American Chicle

John H. Scalise
Eckerd Drug Company

Dotti Schultz
Duracell IDM

Pete Secker
Enesco Corporation

Laura Seitz
Epson America, Incorporated

Graham F. Shackell
W.D. & H.O. Wills (Aust.) Limited

Barbara Shannon
The W.E. Bassett Company

Stephen A. Shapiro
The Gillette Company

Robert Skattum
American Express Company

Geoffrey N. Skog
Allied Signal Automotive Aftermarket

Lois Slachowitz
Chesebrough-Pond's USA

Steve Small
New Zealand Breweries

Barry T. Smith
Anheuser-Busch, Inc.

William Smith
The Procter & Gamble Company

Barbara Sommer
Letraset USA

Robert E. Sorensen
Micromall

Richard W. Spademan
The Glidden Company

Marc Springer
Applause, Incorporated

Jeanne Stall
Fisher-Price, Incorporated

John F. Staples
Flowers Industries, Incorporated

Peggy Stath
Putman Food Group

Pamela Steel
Timex Corporation

Cynthia Stiles
Pleasant Company

Robert M. Stuart
Polaris Pool Systems, Incorporated

John Q. Stumpf
Eastman Kodak Company

Tom Sullivan
R.J. Reynolds Tobacco Company

Mark K. Sundberg
Tambrands, Incorporated

Louis J. Szepi
Hallmark Cards, Incorporated

Charles Tagliareni
Borden, Incorporated

Charles Thomas
The Southland Corporation

M. Pattie Torrence
Continental Baking Company

Michele Torsiello
AT&T

Glenn C. Van Deusen
Bausch & Lomb

Ellen Vanook
Random House Publishers

Daniel T. Vnencak
Nabisco Biscuit Company

Laura M. Ward
Hallmark Cards, Inc.

Jeffrey T. Weber
Planters LifeSavers Company

Jonathan A. Weinstein
Tiffen Manufacturing Corporation

David West
The Star Song Publishing Group

Des Weymark
Rothmans of Pall Mall Australia,
Limited

Randy M. Wheaton
Parfums deCoeur

Charles R. White
Reckitt & Colman, Incorporated

Marcy Whitman
Palm Bay Imports, Incorporated

Vincent R. Wilkins
Congoleum Corporation

Dorothy S. Williams
The Coca-Cola Company

Charles W. Wood
Shaw Industries, Incorporated

Mike Wrobel
William Wrigley Jr. Company

Larry Wurzel
Calico Cottage Candies, Incorporated

Ronald Yonker
Planters LifeSavers Company

Wayne A. York
Heublein, Incorporated/Hart Division

Ted P. Zachary
The Procter & Gamble Company

Jonathan Zelinger
Ethical Products, Incorporated

Aaron Zutler
St. George Crystal, Limited

Michael Zutler
St. George Crystal